Financial Secrets
for the

Man of Means

Warmest Regards

Scott

Financial Secrets

for the

Man of Means

Scott Thomas

 LEGACY Publishing Services
1885 Lee Road, Winter Park, FL 32789
www.LegacyPublishingServices.com

Published by:
LEGACY Publishing Services, Inc.
1885 Lee Road
Winter Park, Florida 32789
LegacyPublishing.Org

Scott Thomas — Registered Representative of and securities offered through QA3 Financial Corp. Member FINRA/SIPC. Investment Advisor Representative of and Advisory Services offered through QA3 Financial, LLC., an SEC Registered Investment Advisory Firm. Financial Farmer Inc. and QA3 are not affiliated companies.

The information contained within is the opinion of the author and not that of any regulatory body or QA3 Financial Corp. The individuals referenced throughout this book have not reviewed its contents nor are their opinions those of any regulatory body for whom they are or were employed.

The dissemination of this material does not constitute a recommendation, solicitation, or offer of the purchase or sale of securities. The material contained in this book is meant to provide information not easily found elsewhere and is intended to help investors formulate their financial opinions in a more objective light.

As with any investment or investment strategy, the outcome depends on many factors, including: investment objectives, income, net worth, tax bracket, risk tolerance, as well as economic and market factors. Before investing or using any investment strategy, individuals should consult with their tax, legal and/or investment advisor.

Dedication

To my wife, Suzanne
and children, Cole, Mason and Abby Grace.
It is because I love you and desire to spend
more time with you that I write this book.

.

PREFACE

I wrote this book for you, The Successful Business Owner: A Man of Means, to encourage you to take action. There are innovative, smart strategies available to grow, protect and harvest maximum benefits to both you and your family. Are you like Sam, who speaks frequently with his investment advisor about stocks and bonds but never about alternative investments? Are you like Jerry, who made over a million dollars in profit in his business and paid taxes all this year? Are you like Tom, who was told that if he wanted to save for retirement he should only consider a SEP-IRA, later to find out he could have doubled the personal deduction and paid only a small fraction of what he paid into the employee SEP-IRA accounts? This book has 44 strategies, written for you in conversational, easy to understand, yet powerful language. I urge you take action today, whether that's reading this book, calling me or contacting your current advisors.

Table of Contents

Introduction

Why do I feel compelled to write a book that does not benefit the masses? My typical client is anything but typical and my approach in using proven strategies is not a mass audience presentation. Rather, it is geared for the Man of Means. What are the secrets? Well they are not secrets to Fortune 500 Corporations nor are they secrets to wealthy individuals that employ enlightened advisors. I did not like the title including the word secrets at first. Many of these secrets were secrets to me 10 years ago when I started on a journey after being asked by a Man of Means to give him feedback on a couple of powerful strategies explained in the first chapter. Why do I spend the time, energy and resources working so hard to produce a book that may become obsolete after a few rounds of tax law changes? Well the opportunity to act on what we have available today is all we can act on, not some future promise on changes. The 44 strategies contained should start a conversation with yourself, and then continue that conversation with your advisors. You will find these ideas to be both brief and easy to understand, especially compared with many of the advanced advisor materials. Writing this book will hopefully allow me more time with my family as a result of being able to direct prospective clients and current clients to specific chapters to educate them before discussing any strategy in detail. My goal is to leverage my time and to clearly share proven strategies by the most efficient method available to meet the planning issues of the Man of Means.

Chapter

CAPTIVES

CAPTIVES

Mr. Highly Successful Business Owner: You have had a team of advisors helping you for several years perhaps. Are you being told there is nothing else you can do about your taxes without giving a large sum of money to your employees? If so, be aware that it may in fact be false or misguided advice. What if I told you that your business may potentially take a high six figure and possibly seven figure deduction to benefit you if you qualify? How would you expect your current advisors to react to information they could have disclosed to you? We suspect they will be a bit defensive. Don't be too hard on them, for they focus on what is being taught in general meetings for the masses, not what is being taught to the affluent of this country. Many advisors are hard working honest people working on your behalf; however, they lack training geared to your issues. They have not ventured to learn what private family offices and trust officers learn. It's possible they don't want to expand their world and they are limiting yours as a result. Sounds cruel? It is what it is. You don't know what you don't know. Let us assume for illustration purposes that over the past five years your business profit, including your salary, was over $500,000 a year. What would it have meant in real dollars if you had paid no federal taxes and later paid only 15% capital gains on most of the money personally paid to you? Let's see: $500,000 at 40% tax rate is $200,000 or a net of $300,000. Over five years that would be over a million dollars in taxes! What if your net worth could use those funds to grow your personal wealth on the money that would have been paid in taxes. What is it worth to you when one of your advisors helps you reduce taxes? What level of expectations do you have for the results of your current planning team and how are those results measured? Would it sound more attractive if we put our fee in a bonded escrow account for a period of time as fully refundable? Would you be surprised to learn that most Fortune 500 Companies have implemented such a plan with enlightened advisors? Ready to learn more? Read on.

The captive insurance industry has grown tremendously over the past 30 years. Tens of thousands of businesses have witnessed great benefits from the use of "captives." With the growth of many foreign and domestic captive domiciles, and a favorable regulatory environment, we believe that there has never been a better time to form and operate a captive.

The U.S. tax law regarding insurance companies and insurance itself dates back over 70 years. Over this period, several key concepts have endured, such as *risk distribution* and *risk transfer*. A third concept that has developed is that the captive insurance must resemble insurance in its traditional sense. These three concepts – risk distribution, risk transfer and "traditional notions" of insurance – form the "core" of the tax law regarding captive insurance.

This chapter contains what we consider to be important areas of the captive insurance tax law as it relates to small and mid-sized businesses. It is not meant to be a substitute for independent review by your tax professional, to help you judge the suitability, risks and operational issues regarding the ownership and operation of an insurance company. We hope that this information will aid the tax professional in such a review. This chapter will address overview, set up and ongoing issues as well as exit strategies. It also will address planning issues and investments within the structure. We will mention other types of captives, but will focus on "parent owned or controlled" and not on group or association plans or rent-a-captive cell companies.

In this section, we will make you aware of many of the various tax issues surrounding captive insurance. Tax law may change over time and so portions of this information may become outdated. We assume no responsibility for updating this data as the law changes. This chapter primarily deals with tax issues regarding captive insurance, although some operational issues are discussed as well. Not all issues regarding the ownership and operation of an insurance company are discussed herein.

While this chapter will outline the tax law and some general principles regarding insurance companies, the application of the law and such principles to any particular captive company is subject to interpretation.

Best Suited

To whom would the following material be appropriate? It is best suited for small and mid-sized companies with cash flow in excess of $500,000 a year. Would you like more money for you and your family? If you are an advisor to such a company, then you will benefit as well.

We will address other aspects of captives in another narrowly focused section in areas such as pooling effects and writing of risks not offered by many insurance carriers. The advantages of access to reinsurance markets and their affect on cash flow and taxes will be looked at as well.

There are some great books on Captives out there that address the why, how,, when and where to set up and massive lists of benefits associated with having multiple captives if you have various needs to address. If your main purpose was to address risks not likely to occur but important nonetheless, then that may very well be a separate captive from self-insuring health or workers compensation. The Man of Means should have access to these financial secrets.

Tax

Among the many benefits of using captives may be some tax benefits. For example, a company that is currently self-funding a layer of exposure for workers' compensation risks may choose to provide for this exposure through a captive. The company could then deduct the premiums paid to the captive, rather than deferring the deduction under the self-funding plan until the claims are actually paid. This gives the business a current tax deduction, rather than a deduction spread out over several years. We have seen individuals with lots of excess cash flow, usually at least $250,000 or more, take large deductions because they also take on lots of risks. The amount of deduction will vary widely depending on the several factors including occupation, vendors, clients, regulations, and other issues. So risks determine a large portion of the deduction. Taxation of captives rules have been on the books over 70 years and the recent changes made in 2001 were clear about one of the popular small company captives. In 2007 we see more interest than ever for the smaller closely held business to consider adapting a captive. In 2006 the Treasury issued a warning to those companies wishing to rent a captive or fund a captive and without taking on the real risk of the others participating. This warning sends a message to the people just trying to use the system to get big deductions without going through analysis and taking on risk associated with those forming the structures.

Taxation is an extremely complex area and professional advice should be sought to protect the interests of shareholders, the insured, and the insurance company. We are fortunate to have access to some of the best captive formation companies and administrators anywhere.

When considering the effect of taxation it is important to look at the different parties that are affected including:

- The insured

- The captive insurance company itself

- The beneficial owners of the captive insurance company

Estate Planning

Another often overlooked benefit would be the advantage to leverage money to children or to grandchildren through properly set exit planning. Assuming you have low claims experience, there are some significant opportunities for estate transfer. Very few books address this important but secondary benefit in utilizing captives.

There is an old Russian proverb that goes like this: "To him that holds a hammer, everything looks like a nail." This can be true in any vocation and it is certainly true with estate planning. The legal field often refers to this as one bailiwick. A bailiwick is defined as one's main vocation and everything else is a distraction. The problem surfaces as a result of those unwilling to continuously learn.

How Captive Fits As Part of Overall Plan

This area is difficult at best and nearly impossible to stay current in terms of overall tax and risk, estate and investment planning. So why do I write a hardback book with materials that will be outdated almost as fast as the ink dries? Well, with web technology, update materials are much easier to come by. Most importantly, more reason to work with a skillful team of advisors working in your best interest.

Writing causes me to stretch and articulate difficult subjects in as simple terms as I can possibly explain. I love creative actions: I love to observe nature and the way God made things that don't make sense to us, yet they work. I like seeing the magic of financial numbers that are logical and applying big picture vision to paint a beautiful outlook with details that will cause a wealthy person to dream new dreams and to see new visions.

When is the best time to read the materials and start a questions journal? Anyone that knows me well knows I am passionate about my journals. Journals are a way I capture thoughts and ideas of others and sometimes a creative way for me to work through issues. We will address a few online resources to assist your research and one place to find a consistent message is to start with www.financialfarmer.com.

Self-Insured or Uninsured

Most business owners fail to recognize that they already self-insure a large amount of risk. Self-insurance without a captive is not deductible for federal and state income tax purposes. However, with a properly structured captive, self-insurance can create substantial current tax deductions. Premiums – previously self-insured – may create legitimate tax deductions that are paid to a captive insurance company.

The most obvious areas of self-insurance include: deductibles and exclusions on existing policies, product warranty/liability, construction defect, mold, subsidence, employment practices, sexual harassment, credit risk associated with accounts receivable, government and administrative actions, and disability.

First Party Claims

What is a first party claim? In essence it's the claim against yourself or your established captive. The above section on self-insured or uninsured states the risk exists whether we recognize it or not. Having established a tax-deductible bucket to deal with the likelihood of claims is what we refer to as a first party claim. If your business has excess cash flow and wishes to safeguard against future losses then a captive may very well be worth considering. Remember that many advisors know little about captives and have no reason to learn about them as they are positioned to provide product and services learned for the mainstream. Many group health insurance agents are familiar with risk retention groups and self-insuring associations that utilize captives, again, a different aspect to captives and one not addressed in this book.

Risk Management

Risk Management and Underwriting Profitability

Conventional insurance is typically provided on a guaranteed cost basis and there is little incentive to improve risk management, as there is no participation in the profitability of the insurance program. However, with a captive insurance company, the parent will benefit from good claims experience, and surplus in the company may be available to the parent by way of dividend. A captive can therefore provide great incentives to improve the risk management philosophy throughout an organization. Recapture of underwriting profits may in fact be one of the biggest reasons to set up a captive. The investment returns inside the captive hold another profit potential along with the ability to choose the risks and pay first party claims (pay yourself or your deductibles). The formula looks like this: Pay premiums, earn investments and experience loss or control losses and make it a profit of the captive. By using a captive, we have seen higher risk occupations and industry shift wealth from the business to personal, or it can help in cleaning up a balance sheet of business positioning to sell and limit a liability.

Risk Retention Group or RRG

Let's say a group of auto dealers wishes to buy coverage not readily available or chooses to take on a higher deductible of catastrophic risk which could wipe out the business. The costs for these types of policies may be cost prohibitive, yet by joining together, they may access a market or have very large deductibles to reduce the cost or maybe obtain higher limits of coverage. Utilizing a retention group may be a wise choice for a more predictable and steady experience of claims.

Administration

Where do you go to get set up and run such an organization? One option is to look at the online resources. CICA is the professional association that educates and helps monitor trends and provides many resources. Their website is www.cica.org. What are the expected setup costs? If domestic, then each state has its filing and annual costs. There are legal formation costs and the field of experienced attorneys in the area is rather limited. We have seen that setup by professionals costs anywhere from $30,000 to $100,000 and then ongoing costs vary from $25,000 to $60,000 a year as of 2007. We would expect you to say, hey that's a big range, and yes we agree and our opinion would be it's a supply and demand function like everything else in life. Most states also charge DAC or deferred acquisition costs taxes on top of filing fees and termination fees. Expecting the captive to be audited every other year seems to be normal. Audits apply to the captive, not your business or personally.

Bring In the Profits and effectively transfer assets to family

It's been my experience that most captives are set up by property and casualty agents and are focused on special risk or tax deduction for deductible or mitigate a risk to the captive. It's very rare that one is set up with the purpose of getting wealth transferred to the personal bottom line or better yet a leverage way to do some very savvy estate planning. We hope that this book will create opportunities to have conversations with highly successful business people getting more wealth to their families.

What does this look like in your business? Premiums paid to captive are tax deductible and reduce business income and wealth is moved to the captive. The captive insurance company has special advantages as an insurance company and the reserves accrue tax-free and many of the profits defer taxes and pay out as long-term capital gains only when distributed.

Currently top tax rates are 20% higher than capital gains rates. Think about this while you can potentially move money from the business to yourself or better yet a trust set up for your family.

Chapter

Getting More Money To Your Heirs

GETTING MORE MONEY TO YOUR HEIRS

We are often asked for all the options afforded to gifting to children and heirs. The following few pages are a brief conversation we hold with clients.

Gifting of Long-Term Care Policy

This may provide additional gifting opportunities for those wishing to fund long-term care liabilities for the next generation while providing a return of premium wealth transfer element. These solutions are exempt from estate and gift tax. There are methods to fund long term care policies with a return of premium provision. So you fund for, say, twenty years at perhaps $10,000 a year and transfer $200,000 additional dollars that do not even count against your current gifting.

Intentional Defective Grantor Trust

Why would anyone want something that is "defective" and how is it defective? The "defective" naming is a result of the trust causing taxes on the trust to be taxable to the grantor, and yet the trust is an asset given away today and fully controlled. Business owners that talk with estate planning attorneys really like the idea of control. Another plus would be the taxes are paid by the grantor outside the trust so the taxes are not included in the estate, thus allowing for more assets to flow to the children or other heirs. What might this look like in practice? Joe and Mary have two daughters that have made less than ideal choices throughout their lives. Joe and Mary love their daughters' spouses, but they are not very hopeful for long-term marriages for various reasons. Joe and Mary's estate is about $5 million and their life-style would not suffer giving away $1 million today. So they put the million now into an Intentional Defective Grantor Trust and the earnings inside the trust continue to grow and are taxed, and Joe and Mary can stroke a check to pay the tax bill. They can also fund another $24,000 a year to the trust for each of their daughters. If the trust earned 6% the first year, the earnings would be $60,000 and, taxed 35%, would be $21,000 in federal taxes also paid by Joe and Mary, thus reducing their the estate, but not the trust. Think of it this way: protection against the himbos and bimbos that wish to marry your children or grandchildren.

Educational gifting

Normally we think about the gift limit of $12,000 a year for children or grandchildren and many do not know that paying tuition expenses paid direct to the institution will not count against the annual gifting limits. This does not include books, room and board. This will not work as a reimbursement to the student. The institution includes any organization whose primary function is formal instruction and which has a regular faculty and curriculum and student body. This could be a trade school, private elementary school or high school or even some extracurricular educational programs. Cooking school, ballet school or sports school are just a few examples of the potential excluded gifting opportunities. Many private institutions rely on this provision to have grandma and grandpa funding the tuition that easily exceeds normal gifting.

Employ your children in the business

If they are young, have them take the trash out and clean the office or do little projects to earn money. IRS says pay should be reasonable and it must really take place. This could be a great way for your teen to earn money and fund a ROTH IRA. We see lots of teens and younger earning a few thousand a year doing all types of work from computer networking to clerical to cleaning to delivery and pickup. There are other benefits potentially available here such as funding a ROTH IRA, maybe a SIMPLE IRA, or a 401(k) plan. If the annual amount of pay is only a few thousand dollars, then think of it this way. Paying the little to no taxes makes a lot of sense in terms of establishing work history, income history for future credit, and federal program qualification, 40 quarters for SSI, and the ability to fund a ROTH, or other earned income programs.

Simple gifting of outright cash or securities

There is a potential problem here with a spouse wishing to cash in on a divorce. If gifting cash, you may wish to have your child open a separate account from the spouse or significant other, in his/her name only. Not that this is always going to help protect the money, but at least the intentional nature was there to gift only to your child, and not the son-in law or daughter-in-law. If protection is your objective, please talk to an attorney about the Intentional Defective Grantor Trust.

If your main concern is to fund after you die, (my estate planning friend express as "when your will matures") then consider funding an Irrevocable Life Insurance Trust a.k.a. ILIT. Another method to consider is the Charitable Lead Trust where you loan to a charity the earnings while you are alive, and then upon death, they revert back to the children or other heirs. Another consideration is, if you primarily want to provide for charity, yet would love to teach your children about sharing and giving, then think about a Donor Advised Fund or Private Family Foundation.

Section 529

529 Plans are another method to not only provide funding for educational costs to your heirs, but they can be an effective estate-planning tool as well. Enlightened advisors will ask you what you wish to accomplish. Some advantages are: Growing assets tax advantaged, controlling

money, beneficiary provisions, and getting money outside the estate. Even adults using these plans provide tax-deferred growth for their grown children or, in some cases, even their parents. Here is the idea behind naming an elderly parent as the beneficiary to such a plan. One, they actually could use it to go back and take some higher education classes. Some take courses abroad or in a hobby field, and are able to effectively grow assets tax free inside the 529 Plan and then use the controls as if it were a family trust. As far as asset protection, we hear many advisors say if within certain listed states then should be protected such as Alaska. On the other hand, we have heard that because 529 Plans are a newer program, the courts in effect have not really tested them according to our attorney friends.

Coverdale Educational IRA
Is an educational program with a low limit of only $2,000 a year and is not designed for serious educational funding. This is not a tax-deductible bucket; however, it operates similar to the ROTH IRA in the sense that it accumulates and distributes tax-free dollars with some limitations. Parents, grandparents, and other relatives sometimes like establishing a tax-free bucket with low costs to operate. There is a donor limit in regards to income as well $170,000 AGI for 2007.

Captives Insurance Company
Could be owned by a trust that has children as beneficiaries and this is the most powerful tax strategy we see as possible for the highly successful business owner. The movement of assets to leverage the trust with tax-deductible dollars from the business can be accomplished. If you passed on the Captives chapter then go back and read it now. It may greatly impact your family's wealth.

Dynasty Trust, a.k.a. Multiple Generations Trust
The idea here is to place money into a bucket without the objective being payout of a lump sum, but

rather having trustees pay for health, welfare, education and maintenance. The trustee determines the needs which are spelled out in a document and this is one of the hottest documents being set up today for wealthy families. We believe it's due to many reasons, including but not limited to: no estate taxes for all future generations, controls in place today to reflect values to future generations, building real monetary legacy for future generations to remember you, and protection of the assets. Many states have passed special laws to allow for hundreds of years without state estate taxes and protection of assets. This is a complicated document and should not be entered into with an inexperienced attorney. This is not basic estate planning and getting the best professional is highly recommended. There are two networks of attorneys we have found to be very strong in helping you find these types of attorneys. One is the National Network of Estate Planning Attorneys located at www.nnepa.org and The Wealth Counsel www.wealthcounsel.org. The trust company you choose needs to be a competitive one and not necessarily the biggest or the one with the better-known name. Often smaller trust companies may offer more competitive fees and are more flexible in regard to using your team of enlightened advisors. Having your advisors informed, and even able to participate in the money management, might be a huge advantage. We are seeing more individuals consider this type of trust for a couple of reasons. First, being in control of the assets to see to it that the money will last and not be used up by the next generation from over self-indulgence. And next, as a powerful means of asset protection and security for future generations, to provide funds for the values and disciplines the donor seeks to promote.

Doing Well While Doing Good
Estate Planners tells us that one of their favorite meetings is showing their clients and prospective clients how being charitable to qualified charities can actually provide more money to their heirs. There are a few ways

this happens. One is leaving qualified retirement accounts to charity and replacing those funds with life insurance outside the touch of estate taxes. Another way to accomplish this would be gifting income today through either a charitable lead trust, or simple charity assignment of income assets, and thereby avoiding taxes and phase-outs in charitable contributions. How could this be done in a practical sense? We assume you are in the top tax bracket because you are reading this book. Instead of earning investment returns and paying ordinary income taxes of 35%+ and then giving money to a charity, you may opt to assign the income to the charity and the charity's tax identity number. Now the charity gets the income direct from investment or certificate of deposit and no taxes paid. An example would look like this: $100,000 earning 6% or $6,000 a year and if paying the average rate of 40% taxes, that would reduce the income by $2,400 or a net of $3,600 to gift. Now, due to phase-outs in charitable gifts, the U.S. Treasury allows maybe 25% of the $3,600 gift or only allows a deduction of $900 on the initial investment earning of $6,000. So why not consider assigning the income for the $100,000 directly to the charity and they pay zero tax and get the use of $6,000 versus only $3,600? If your advisors are bringing these kinds of ideas to add value to your family and charitable causes, then you are a blessed man and we recommend you tell your advisors "thank you" for learning about the little stuff that adds up to be significant.

Chapter

Leveraged Bonus Plan

LEVERAGED BONUS PLAN

With recent changes in the law (namely the Sarbanes-Oxley Act of 2002) and with corporate failures, companies are struggling for new ways in which to reward and retain key executives. In response to stock option plans being underwater and/or an increased focus on the general creditor risk in non-qualified retirement plans, another strategy is called The "Leveraged Bonus Plan" (LBP), another term for Premium Finance. Premium Finance is a term widely used to find a method to borrow money on the corporate level and then use the proceeds to fund insurance purchases of all types (workers compensation, liability, life insurance on buy sell agreements, etc.)

The LBP is an executive benefits strategy allowing a company to fully deduct all contributions to the program while providing the executive participants with full benefit security on the dollars contributed to the plan.

Why the LBP?

When companies evaluate traditional non-qualified plan options, they soon discover the significant drawbacks that exist when utilizing a non-qualified plan: (1) company and employee contributions are not deductible, (2) participants are "at risk" and are general creditors to the company, and (3) the business owners have to accrue a plan liability on the books for 30-plus years. The LBP solves all of these concerns.

What are the Advantages?

- Generally, company contributions are tax-deductible

- Little ongoing accounting, record keeping or administration issues

- Participant may receive a secured benefit as opposed to being a general creditor to the company, assuming it is funded properly

- Opportunity to earn equity returns with no equity market risk for invested dollars depending on the product selection

We don't like using terms like, "generally", "little impact", "may receive" and "opportunity or potential for big gain". All of these are, of course, disclaiming back out language, and frankly, there are wonderful benefits here. Unfortunately, they are often botched with wild promises or claims, and then you find out the truth of the matter is that they must be structured in a very specific fashion. Often you will find that asset protection of assets is a byproduct of another business use and tax-deductible expenses are a byproduct of the U.S. Treasury encouraging business owners and individuals to act in a particular fashion, or take on certain responsibilities.

Plan Structure

The Company provides a tax-deductible bonus program that allows each participant to fund the leveraged bonus plan. The Plan allows the employees to make net pre-tax contributions to the program with similar benefits when compared to a non-qualified deferred compensation plan. The result of the Plan is deductible cash flow for the owners and full benefit security for the participants. The LBP is ideally suited for the small to mid-sized privately held company.

The Accounts Receivable Financing Arrangement

What is accounts receivable financing and how should it work?

This area is especially hot market for physicians who often have very high accounts receivables. In fact, we have often seen this as the largest asset of many specialist physicians. There are a few turnkey accounts receivable companies that package the loans with life insurance. Often the providing vendor of the loan has only a couple of companies they work with and they receive substantial amounts of commissions in the form of overrides. The advisor is reduced to a worker bee bringing the honey back to the hive for the queen bee.

Any business with large amounts of accounts receivable on the books knows that this is classified as a working asset according to the accountants. As a practical matter, however, it's a stagnant non-productive asset. Lots of factoring companies are quick to point out this fact, and offer an opportunity to get the money now, and get it working in your business.

What should be the objectives of the Accounts Receivable finance arrangement?

1) Asset Protection from lawsuits

2) Moving a non-working asset to a productive asset

It is very important to counsel with local legal advice in this area, as each state is different in what is protected and what would be allowed. For example a UCC1 (banking term for Unified Commercial Credit first lien on assets) filing may be unprotected for a period of one year in one state and in others are protected one day prior to claim. The last thing you want is to start something that will lock you into payments for five years, paying high interest rates and high life insurance costs, and then not protecting the asset you worked so diligently to secure.

The "Premium Finance" is similar in that both buy an insurance product. Premium Finance is focused on tax deductions or buying insurance on a tax favored basis. Accounts Receivable Plans are generally focused on asset protection with a UCC1 filing stripping away the asset. Don't expect a tax deduction for interest on the loan. It's a personal loan secured by business assets. The proceeds of the loan purchase a life insurance policy, which in most states is also a protected asset. Annuities also work. However, due to the differing tax structure on the distributions, life policies are more tax efficient. Life policies' tax-free distribution in the form of loans is the difference. Get your team communicating on the structure and what are the main objectives.

This is a complicated subject that can turn bad for the business owner if not properly structured. Be careful here. There are several items that can go wrong. Here are a few warnings and one solution to this potentially viable strategy.

If the salesperson states your interest on the loan is deductible as factual, then beware. If you utilize a "Back To Back" Loan arrangement, then the employee must have made capital contributions in order to show offsetting losses and have deductible interest. Without capital contributions this can be done, but it will compromise the asset protection aspect of the program and one would be better off to simply do a personal loan and apply an interest charge to the individual. Another aspect that gets confusing on many plans is: who is the owner of the policy? If a corporation is the owner then the tax buildup or growth in the policy would be taxable and generally not asset protected. If the individual is the owner and the business takes out the loan, and the claim by the promoter is a back-to-back loan, then there had better be a contributed basis. Rules state that back-to-back loans in these arrangements must have the following: who needs to have contributed or placed actual money into the business rather than the idea of earn out or over a period of time buying into the practice.

Potential Solution

Have the individual acquire the loan based on individual and company financials and personal guarantee. The life policy is purchased on the individual and it cannot be used for "key man" insurance. If used in a buy/sell funding, the proceeds from the life insurance may be taxable. Remember to update the corporate resolution to reflect the ability to utilize Accounts Receivables and equipment to help officers acquire or secure a personal loan. Consult your accountant. If the policy is purchased by the company used for estate and personal reasons, then the individual should pay the corporation the Federal Funds Rate FFR for the loan extended to the employee. There should be an employment agreement in place to address this issue so other employees do not require similar treatment. Our understanding here would create income tax on the entire loan. Another method would be to set up another corporation specifically for the life policy arrangement and accounts receivable and get more complicated. The lending institution will require a way to collateralize the loan beyond the corporation due to the individual's owning the policy. Maybe some bankers are too kind and diplomatic to say that the insurance agent's promises are twisted, and tax counsels review would review other such problems as taxation on corporate-owned polices and even the yearly buildup on such plans if improperly structured. Best case again, use premium finance for liabilities in the business and use personal loans with a UCC lien as asset protection.

Chapter

FUTURE
HEALTHCARE
COSTS

FUTURE HEALTHCARE COSTS

Future Healthcare Costs

The US Government has projected that our nation's healthcare spending will increase by +6.9% annually over the next decade. Inflation has increased +2.7% over the last decade (source: Financial Times, Department of Labor).

Would it not be a better choice to get a tax deduction today for future medical costs and get access to the money for such expenses in the future, all 100% tax free? Can such a bold proposal be available? The answer is empathically yes, and not only this, but there are three different ways to accomplish it now.

Health Reimbursements Arrangements or HRA

Just say the words "health insurance" and the average small business owner might start hyperventilating. This reaction is totally understandable considering the draconian rules and codes required of any small business owner who wants to provide reasonable health care for his or her employees without going broke along the way.

Fortunately, there are four solutions that entrepreneurs can implement immediately to get tax-deductible dollars today. Some of you may already be familiar with Health Savings Accounts, or HSAs, as they're commonly known. HSAs typically allow $5500 annual per family tax deduction into a savings account. The second solution is less well known but can be a real boon to tax deduction dollars. It's known as an HRA or Health Reimbursement Arrangement.

Health Reimbursement Arrangements are tax-deductible accounts that allow employers to pre-fund, or fund from an ongoing account, monies to reimburse all or a portion of an employee's medical expenses. It works in concert with any existing health insurance plan as well as HSAs, and is not only a tax deduction for the employer but also non-taxable income to the employee.

Using HRAs can help small business owners in several ways. It can help make employees more aware of their health care options, it can allow for a raise in deductibles since the HRA can match the difference in the deductible increase, and it can help an employer offer more compelling health care coverage without having to affect the wages of employees. When you combine the employer tax-friendly nature of HRAs, they can be a terrific option for any small business owner looking to offer the best quality care. It's a win-win situation, which is a real rarity when it comes to insurance.

Traditionally, HRAs are paper-only arrangements. The employer doesn't incur any expense associated with the HRA until an employee has a claim, unless they choose to pre-fund the account, which would offer a tax advantage and no need for "out of pocket" spending when a claim arises. An HRA also allows the employer to control the level of annual rollover of leftover funds. What would a tax-deductible bucket of money with tax-free distributions for future medical and insurance needs mean to you as the employer? This might be the benefit that attracts the right kinds of employees to grow your business.

The HRA plans can be implemented three ways, either as a first dollar plan, an employee pays first plan, or by split employee/employer payments. The plans can't be cashed out, which allows for their non-taxable nature and employees can use them not only for themselves, but for their families as well. With all this customization HRAs can blend seamlessly with any current medical coverage.

Third method of funding benefits for the current year is called the "Flexible Spending Account" a.k.a.

FSA. Some of you know them as cafeteria plans or Section 125 flexible benefits accounts. It's a great way to reduce FICA and Medicare Taxes as well as the federal taxes. This is not a new program. They have been around since the 1970s and most large employers have them. According to Mercer Human Resource Consulting, only about one-third of the smaller companies (those less than 500 employees) have FSAs. These have become easier with debt cards and end-of-year carryover for up to two and a half months. This has eased the "use it or lose it" rules. Were you aware that over the counter drugs are now allowed? So you could load up on supplies like prescription sunglasses, acne treatment, pain relievers, antacids, hearing aid batteries, shoe inserts, and cough/cold medicines. Take another look at this powerful benefit.

We recently learned that it's possible to combine HRA with HSA and FSA and have rules in place to customize employees' benefits. There are some very compelling reasons to think outside the box here. One is to create a bucket of money, say 25% of payroll, and then allow employees to choose from perhaps three different medical plans to fit the employees' needs. Next you allow for employee-saved money to be utilized in FSA for maximum tax benefits. The employees like the choices of whether to buy a benefits rich plan or sock away dollars for high deductible or some combination. They may be partial to vision and dental benefits over having a low deductible. The point here is that not all employees will see your pre-selected plan as beneficial to them and their wants and needs.

Think of the flexible spending account as the year's best way to fund short-term expenses and known premium costs on a tax-deductible basis. So, suppose the employee decides at the beginning of the year to fund $3,000 to cover costs for this year, including the family co-pay, vision premiums and dental on a pre-tax basis (savings potential $1279) 35% federal, 7.65% other taxes. Not only federal but also FUTA FICA SUTA Medicare taxes as well. Let's say for illustration purposes that your spouse works for a company either part-time or full-time and has access to such a plan. Your spouse could save at your Federal Tax rate and get deductions for Medicare and FUTA FICA SUTA or an additional 7.65% and if there is a State Income Tax then there is a saving there as well. Why have our tax laws looked so favorably on FSA, HRA and HSA? We have a healthcare crisis here with rates growing out of hand and a big need for funding medical costs. Healthcare reform will require more than a few tax breaks to solve the issues at hand.

Another possible solution in the quest to reduce healthcare costs is to reduce the claims costs with small claims on low deductible plans. One possible solution could be a model introduced in Florida in the form of employer-centered clinic and doctor visits and prescription included for a managed one low cost. Ohio has a similar program working well. Costs for these plans can be a fraction of traditional health policies. These same clinics could offer services similar to an emergency room or other urgent care facilities during the evening hours. With Medicare cutting reimbursement costs to emergency rooms at hospitals, many hospitals will be looking for ways to defer less complicated services to more efficient models. The employer would contract directly with the clinic to provide all basic services and then major hospitalizations would be covered with an insured catastrophic plan. The clinic plan married with the catastrophic plan should yield sufficient savings from what is currently being offered in most communities. Technology will help drive down health care costs for claims made without any paperwork. One would just present a "smart" medical card with records and automatic filing for small claims. Maybe this is the first time you have heard about this concept that is a reality in some parts of this country.

We could go on and on about all the potential drivers like legal costs, and soft costs associated to document everything. The purpose for mentioning this study above and the low dollar high frequency claims issue is that we need to think differently. Move towards higher deductibles and look to special arrangements with lower cost provider clinics to take care of the rank and file employees. Some believe this can only be solved on a national level while others see that local arrangements will deliver faster and more efficient services for those employers concentrated in a smaller geographic area.

Lastly, we as employers should encourage healthy habits in the workplace and outside the workspace. Wellness programs including weight loss and smoking cession and gym memberships with incentives have been shown to be effective.

VEBA or Voluntary Employee Beneficiary Associations
The fourth way to address future funding is called a VEBA in which funding is discretionary and allows employers to fully deduct payments for future funding or they may simply create a liability for future medicals and specify in the document what would and would not be covered. This is a protected asset and falls under ERISA law. Funding is discretionary and not limited as in retirement plans. Some advisors get VEBAs and Welfare Benefits Trust confused. Both have dealings with Section 419 of the tax code. The VEBAs can get IRS determination letters and the "deferred compensation" 419(a)f(6) will not get such a letter from the Service. Your advisors should tell you that Private Letter Rulings are okay, but not as strong as pre-determined letter by the Service. One is the opinion of lawyers and the other is a stamp of pre-approval from the Service. In 2002, a pair of rulings stomped the 419 plans and made them almost useless unless narrow rules for Unions apply to an employer. VEBAs have been around since the 1920s and there have been several types popular and then later misused and changed. VEBAs are powerful tools for employers to fund deductible dollars and provide benefits in the future. These will not work for every company. There is a suitable place, though, where maybe 10-25 employees wishing to fund benefits and needing tax

breaks now and tax-free benefits in the future are excellent candidates for this plan. Find someone on your team willing to explore and test your company censes and personal objectives for a proper fit. The key areas for VEBA may be estate tax funding of Life Insurance Trust, Funding Buy Sell Agreement with deductible dollars, or simply flexible plan. There are a lot more things to be said about VEBAs but for the sake of simplicity I will stop short of giving many of the details. Currently VEBAs have a few interesting provisions related to fund and distribution. Very high levels can be funded. For instance, a mature business owner wants to fund $50,000 this year and zero the following year and maybe $100,000 after that and without ongoing commitments.

Tax reporting for the VEBA uses Form 990 and Form 5500. Form 990 is considered to be much easier than a 1040 and having a good administration to handle the 5500 makes these plans easy to maintain. Remember you can pick and choose the level and when you wish to fund such a plan. Employers who have been told that their current pension is over-funded and that they can no longer contribute are also excellent candidates for a VEBA. The premise for deductions comes under the ordinary and necessary business expense in Section 162 of the Internal Revenue Code.

Are the VEBAs protected from creditors? Yes. Like other ERISA plans, this plan has an independent trustee not under the control of the participants and therefore is a good asset protection vehicle. No creditors will be able to attach to the VEBA. So highly compensated business owners with high risk are excellent candidates for this plan if they wish to fund future medical benefits or purchase life insurance on a pre-tax basis. There is no vesting of employees so you don't give away benefits to ex-employees, and funds should not be subject to divorce decree as in retirement plans that do vest. Consult your tax and legal team on the proper structure here. Realize there are a lot of resources available to your team in the way of lawyers on retainer at the administration level. Experts are necessary in unique settings.

If your objective is only to purchase a supplemental retirement plan, then consider a 412(i) that uses fixed life and annuity products. We have seen business owners laugh at these conservative plans for low fixed returns; however, they usually smile when reviewing the amount of tax deductions allowed under the plans. Conservative may fit well as the safe play among high risk and aggressive investors. Do not discount the plan because of the lower fixed returns. One word of caution here to business owners: Get multiple quotes and manage the expenses or load going into these products because there is little to nothing you can do about the rates being credited to the plans. Interest rates credited are all about the same.

We will address these plans in the chapter on retirement plans.

Chapter

RETIREMENT PLANS

RETIREMENT PLANS

If you're a high income earning and not high net worth then tax deductible retirement plans are well suited to help you build wealth. If however, your net worth is over say $2 million and growing then a retirement plan may not be in your best interest. If you're the latter you may skip down to the section titled "IRD".

Three critical issues we see in regard to small successful employers are:

1) Wrong plan type, not allowing large enough contribution

2) Investments are not well planned to take advantage of tax deferral feature

3) Little to no thought regarding the future distributions.

For simplicity, we generally see the adoption of two employer plans: SEP IRA or SIMPLE IRA.

SEP is a special type of individual retirement account and, as its name implies, Simplified Employee Pension (SEP) it is easy to understand. Owners of the business may contribute up to 25% of their payroll for the employees. The limit for 2007 is $45,000. Who are these eligible employees? Anyone who has earned more than $450 in the past three of five years. So, an employer that decides to contribute 15% into the plan must include these employees as well. This seems to be the most popular for single or very small employers. There are some notable limits we will address in this chapter.

SIMPLE (IRA) is a Savings Incentive Match Plan for Employees. It is similar to the 401(k) and only for employers with 100 or less employees. The upper limits are $15,500 for those over age 50 and $11,000 for those less than 50 years of age for the elected employee deferral. The employer can either elect to give all employees 2% or match employees up to 3% with 100% match. We see a nice fit for those employers not wishing to fund big dollars and having an inexpensive plan to set up and keep, assuming other employees are either not contributing or there is high turnover rate. Eligible employees are those with $5000 or so in wages and expecting to have the same in the next year. Excluded for up to two years and we see most only exclude for the first year. There is no 5500 reporting and no testing like 401(k) plans. Because there is no vesting schedule, that means the employees own the match and walk with the matching dollars when they leave or cash out. These plans are very expensive if your company has lots of turnover. However, for those only looking for moderate funding levels and no participation from employees, this is a winner.

Because you are reading this book, we should first congratulate you on your success and next tell you that if you truly wish to maximize your tax deductions and funding towards retirement then you should consider another type of plan.

There are basically two types of vesting tax-deductible retirement plans: Defined Benefit (DB) and Defined Contribution (DC) plans. The DBs are employer-funded pensions and the DCs are employee-driven, such as the 401(k) profit sharing plans. Now these plans can be combined in light of the 2006 Pension Protection Act and may in fact be the most advantageous for you, the successful business owner looking for the big tax effect and the most money in your pocket. We like to refer to his "Hip National Bank," or what goes to you personally.

The Defined Benefit Plans are based on age, salary and funded to reach a set benefit of perhaps $12,000 a month when employees reach age 62 or 65. Retirement plans continue to change in the amounts that individuals can contribute and the percentage of income that employers can place into employees' tax deferred buckets. Important note: These buckets of money will indeed be taxed in the future, hence the name "tax deferred." What might tax rates be in the future compared to today? Consider, in the final analysis, putting into the plan a few "what ifs," such as pay the tax today and grow into a long term capital gain bucket like real estate or index fund of stocks or some of the other tax sensitive strategies discussed in this book. Another consideration is that the size of your future estate and the amount of dollars inside retirement plans will adversely affect your family financial picture in a greater way than non-retirement benefits. If your estate planning team is honest with you, they would encourage you not to place more money inside these structures that tax defer and create lots of pain for family seeing 70+% going to lump sum taxes upon your death. The enlightened advisors will suggest that if you are pushing hard for tax deductions, then take the DB plan funding and pair it up with $20,500 into ROTH 401(k) which is 100% tax free in earnings and tax free in distributions. The ROTH 401(k) is new, only introduced in 2001, and the first plans were started January 2006. It was not until the Pension Protection Act and some clarifications were made the end of 2006 that many started understanding the powerful savings potential of tax-free. The stand alone ROTH has income limits of $170,000 AGI for 2007. The ROTH 401(k) does not look at income limits at all! Ask your team or at least your attorney if they agree with the idea of not adding to the retirement plan in order to provide for your family. They should cite Required Minimum Distributions a.k.a. RMD as forced distributions and forced taxes upon obtaining age 70 ½ or they should cite Income Respect to Decedent a.k.a. IRD, the double tax whammy few discuss and, because you are successful, is very likely to occur. The Man of Means may be better off not using tax-deductible dollars. To not max fund your 401K and max fund your retirement dollars for deductions today goes against most advisors.

RMD starts off with distributions based on percentage of the prior years end value. For example, at age 71, married with spouse within ten years of the individual's age: utilizes the Uniform Lifetime Table. The percentage of distribution required at 71 is 3.78% and at age 80, it is 5.35%. At age 90, it is 8.78% and at age 95, it is 12.35%. Get the idea? Okay, what if you are single and take distributions? Then the 71-year-old is 6.14% and the 95-year-old is 24.39%.

IRD

IRD works this way: When you pass away, your estate has various items calculated to determine the items called "preference" that are subject to taxes (federal, state and estate) and guess what? The taxes paid here are not reducing the estate taxes and therefore are creating a tax item that gets double taxes. We have seen historically some estate pays 70-80+% taxes on these items. If you have an enlightened team working on your behalf, then these issues can be proactively addressed with alternative solutions laid before you. Be sure that if you do inherit money from someone other than your spouse that if there was an IRD applied then you as the beneficiary get to take the taxes paid as a deduction. We see this as one of the bigger mistakes made on distributions.

A few terms to know when discussing plan any of the plans: vesting, matching, safe harbor, discretionary, Form 5500.

Do you have or want a plan to benefit the employees primarily or is it for you to sock away the most for you? How you answer this question will be critical to the type of plan and another question that needs to follow is do you wish for a moderate contribution $10,000+ and large contribution $45,000+ or a jumbo contribution $100,000+ for yourself?

SIMPLE IRA and 401(k) are designed for moderate contribution in general and the "New Cash Balance Define

Benefit Plans" are designed for jumbo contributions. The large maybe a SEP or 401(k) with Profiting sharing or some other provisions like cross testing.

Traditional 401(k) and Safe Harbor Provision Plans.
Often, when we explain to employers (smaller, under 100) the costs of administration and compliance and limitations, they opt for no plan or SIMPLE IRA. For owners to find a nice benefit usually requires age-weighted and cross-tested plans. There is a method by which the determination for the majority of funding goes to the older owners with higher incomes above $92,000 for tax year 2007. If looking for moderate contribution $45,000 and low contribution for staff then ideally the highest compensated and oldest is the owner and everyone else is several years younger and paid much less.

Some ideal business people for the Defined Benefit Plan would include older/ highly compensated individuals. Examples would be solo consultants, a smaller company where most are younger, or even a university professor with a second income.

Example: 57-year-old male playing catch up and is currently doing SEP Plan. Average W-2 income of $232,000. Can contribute $195,487 in 2007 vs. only $45,000 into the SEP Plan. In a 40% marginal rate, only saves $18,000 on combined federal and state income taxes. DB Plan would save $78,000.

Since Qualified plans seem to change quite a bit every few years, having a review is not only prudent but may create a significant liability for your business if not properly re-evaluated and reviewed. The Pension Protection ACT, EGGTRA were the last two major overhauls in the Employee Retirement arena.

Pension Protection Act (PPA)
Increases Defined Benefit (DB) plan deduction limits and repeals combined deduction limit when combining DB with Defined Contribution for most individuals.

If funding a DC for 6% or less, then maximize DB contribution for 2007 plans. These plans used to be limited to the 25% rule.

If the employer contributions to the DC plan do exceed the 6%, then the new combined limit of 31% of compensation applies and after 2007 the combined limit does not apply.

One Strategy

Strategy One: Emphasize the DB

Employer can contribute 6% to satisfy top heavy and safe harbor rules and this allows highly compensated to max fund their DB plan.

A DB plan is designed to maximize the contributions to the owner(s).

The defined benefit plan can be traditional, tiered and/or cash balance.

- Traditional/Tiered are based upon historical salary averages

- This creates a required annual contribution even if the compensation drops, while

- Cash balance plans are normally written as a percent of current compensation, so if comp drops, so does the contribution

- Easy to communicate to employees in terms of deposits and what is owed upon retirement or termination

DB is Primary Plan / Strategy One

	Age	Comp	Tiered DB	ER Deposit	Deferrals	Totals
HCE1	55	225,000	115,857	6,750	20,500	143,107
HCE2	42	110,000	30,995	6,050	15,500	52,545
HCE3	41	100,000	30,995	5,500	15,500	51,995
Subtotal		435,000	177,847	18,300	51,500	247,647
NHCE1	35	80,000	3,999	4,400	0	8,399
NHCE2	32	65,000	3,249	3,575	0	6,824
NHCE3	29	50,000	2,500	2,750	0	5,250
NHCE4	39	45,000	2,250	2,475	0	4,725
NHCE5	27	45,000	2,250	2,475	0	4,725
NHCE6	24	30,000	1,500	1,650	0	3,150
Subtotal		315,000	15,748	17,325	0	33,073

Strategy Two: Owner maxes the DC side and puts the difference into the DB plan.

- Maximize the ER contributions to the Defined Contribution plan for the owner(s) and fund the DB with the difference:

- Maximize the contribution to the owners under a PS or 401(k) plan,

- Compute the percentage of ER contribution as a % of compensation

- Subtract this amount from 31%.

The difference is the contribution to the DB plan.

In addition to designing plans individually to use the new limits, one can combine the plans using permissive "aggregation," thus testing both plans as one plan.

This helps pass coverage and discrimination tests while often reducing the amount given to rank and file.

SEP IRAs are not always good. Some push SEP because it's simple. They don't have enlightened advisors in the retirement planning area.

- It takes $180,000 of W-2 compensation to get to $45,000 in a SEP

- It takes $118,000 of W-2 compensation to get to $45,000 in a 401(k)

- It takes the following W-2 compensations to get to $45,000 in a DB/DC Combo arrangement

Age 40, $112,250
Age 45, $75,000
Age 50, $46,500
Age 55, $29,500
(No compensation = No required contribution!)

DC is Primary Plan / Strategy Two

	Age	Comp	Tiered DB	ER Deposit	Deferrals	Totals
HCE1	55	225,000	115,219	29,500	20,500	165,219
HCE2	42	110,000	1,908	14,300	15,500	31,708
HCE3	41	100,000	1,715	13,000	15,500	30,215
Subtotal		435,000	118,842	56,800	51,500	227,142
NHCE1	35	80,000	879	7,200	0	8,079
NHCE2	32	65,000	543	5,850	0	6,393
NHCE3	29	50,000	343	4,500	0	4,843
NHCE4	39	45,000	617	4,050	0	4,667
NHCE5	27	45,000	291	4,050	0	4,341
NHCE6	24	30,000	161	2,700	0	2,861
Subtotal		315,000	2,834	28,350	0	31,184

- One Person Design
- Combination of Defined Benefit Plan: Traditional or Cash Balance with a Defined Contribution Plan designed to maximize contributions, the greater of:
31% of compensation ($69,750 for 2007) plus 401(k) salary deferrals, or

6% of compensation plus salary deferrals in a 401k plan plus 100% of compensation in the cash balance plan limited by 415 (can be greater than 31%)

The chart below shows some ways age and higher income are impacted when looking to increase the benefits to you the business owner.

Name	Cash Balance Contribution	Profit Sharing Contribution	401 (k) Contribution	Totals
Up to 31% of Compensation - $225,000				
Owner 30	37,620*	29,500	15,500	82,620
Owner 35	40,250*	29,500	15,500	85,250
6% plus cost of DB - Comp at $225,000				
Owner 40	64,260	13,500	15,500	93,260
Owner 45	83,985	13,500	15,500	112,985
Owner 50	109,765	13,500	20,500	143,765
Owner 55	143,458	13,500	20,500	177,458
*actual number subject to 415 limitation				

- The following designs are for a client with one major owner, two minor shareholders plus six rank and file employees.

Strategy One emphasizes the DB plan and gives as much as possible to all three HCEs.

- A safe harbor 401(k) plan is added but limited to 6% of total compensation or less.

Strategy Two

Strategy Two emphasizes the DC plan first; the remaining deductible limit is used to design a tandem DB plan targeting the majority owner.

- Combination of a Cash Balance Plan and Safe Harbor 401(k) Plan

The cash balance shown is 51.50% of compensation for HCE1, 28% for HCE2, 31% for HCE3 and 5% for the rest of employees.

The 401(k) plan is designed to give all employees (including HCE1) the 3% safe harbor plus 2.5% to everyone except HCE1.

- Strategy One gives more as a percentage of pay to all the HCEs. The design shown just happens to be under 31% of total compensation; however, if contributions to the Cash Balance plan increase causing the combined total to go over the 31% contribution limit, this is not a problem as long as the ER Contributions to the DC plan stay at 6% or less.

- Strategy Two is weighted more heavily to the majority owner. The combination of these plans must stay under 31% of pay, so if the DB's contributions increase, the DC contributions must decrease accordingly.

- Salary Deferrals - $15,500

- Catch-ups - $5,000 for those over 50 years of age

- Simple Deferral limits - $10,500

- Catch-ups for Simples - $2,500 for those over 50

- DC Limit - $45,000 annual additions

- Compensation Limit - $225,000

- Highly Compensated - $100,000

- Key Employee - $145,000

- Taxable Wage Base - $97,500

Early we said that there is a 50% penalty for over funding a retirement plan or failing to take the Required Minimum Distribution. Here is one strategy that can help in this area. It's called IRA Maximization or IRA Max and can be very effective if you are healthy and/or spouse is healthy and you want to leave money to your family. Here is how the strategy can work: Identify a portion and reposition it in the following way. Invest this portion into a Single Premium Immediate Annuity (SPIA), which provides a lifetime income. The income from the SPIA is taxable income without penalties. Use the after tax proceeds here to purchase life insurance and the owner is either the children or a life insurance trust. Either one of these will not be subject to estate taxes provided a total per beneficiary per spouse per year is maintained.

What is happening here is elimination of federal taxes to the family, using the SPIA it's taxed now, not in addition to estate taxes later on. There is no estate taxation for heirs and assets are protected with a life insurance trust, if utilized. Beneficiaries prefer cash not subject to taxes or probate. This method could also work with annuities that grow tax deferred and create similar problems to IRA.

Solo 401(k) or Individual 401(k)

Allow up to $100,000 tax deductible. Contribution differs based on assumed rate of return. Some actuaries are too conservative or too aggressive in investment returns. We see solo 401(k) often provides more contributions than SEP-IRA.

Chapter

FREEZE YOUR ASSETS

FREEZE YOUR ASSETS

Is this legal? Yes. Why would anyone want to freeze his assets? Maximize gifts to children and other family members. Often we get asked if this will require one to gift away assets to charities. This is not about charity, unless you are one that says charity begins at home, and it means keeping more in the family. There are charitable methods for reducing your estate and we will address those later.

One benefit would be if you could identify a greatly appreciating asset(s) and then place this inside a special type of Family Limited Partnership or FLP. The difference in this type vs. the traditional FLP is that there are two classes of stock shares established. "Common" shares and "preferred" shares classes. Common interest will be subordinated to the preferred in voting and distribution rights. What happens next involves the division of shares, say, 50/50 to the two classes and then upon future liquidation the preferred, due to the unique nature, would have perhaps 10% of the total distribution and the remainder would flow to the common interest.

For example: Fund a FLP with $3 million puts $1.5 million into preferred and $1.5 million into common, and the assets grow to $6 million over the next seven years. Upon distribution, the preferred interest would be 10% of the FLP or $150,000 income interest, and the remaining balance would be a gift to the heirs. In other words $5,850,000 is transferred to the heirs without taxes, and without buying life insurance and placing money in a life insurance trust.

Another option would be to leave some money in the partnership to purchase a life insurance policy. There would be a tax on the distribution left inside the partnership and the partnership could pay the taxes on the distribution. Let's say there was $100,000 left in the partnership. The taxes would be approximately $30,000.

Okay, now let's say you want to super charge the process. Son is 10% preferred and mother is 90% limited. There are some powerful ways to have a Family Limited Partnership and Life Insurance on each to fund. The mother's estate valuation is based on the position of her interest, discounted perhaps 10% of the value of the son's preferred life insurance policy. See the following projection to see the potential of such a strategy. Advisors who get this idea are not only enlightened, but also creative enough to see beyond the normal process of using basic legal documents to protect and provide for heirs more efficiently.

Projected value of ownership interest in mother's estate at the time of formation and purchase of the preferred life insurance policy:

At a 6% discount	$6,692,614
At a 8% discount	$2,510,710
At a 10% discount	$1,815,664
At a 12% discount	$925,210
At a 14% discount	$464,209

Charity

Another possible way to freeze your estate or at least control the growth of assets inside your estate is through the use of Charitable Trusts. Many wealthy families are charitable, and give or assign the income from assets today for a period of time, and then the principal flows to the heirs. Nice in the sense that investments that would be taxable, and then are passed on in the form of check writing to a charity, would not be subject to taxes. To earn high yields and flow them through to a charity tax-free is a beautiful thing.

What if you are phased out on your charitable deductions (personal tax return and assume your business is not a C Corporation) and yet you desire to give today to your favorite causes. The assignment of a taxable high yielding investment may be just the thing to flow money to a "qualified charity" corporation. You don't have to pay the taxes due on the investments because the investments have been assigned to flow through to charity. A $100,000 with 8% higher yield corporate bond would flow $4,000 every 6 months, or $8,000 a year, to a named charity. The charity gets the cash flow and pays no taxes on the income. The individual has the right to get the principal back in a couple of years for family benefit or heirs. If the individual invested in high yield investments and had to pay federal and state income taxes, then did not get a deduction due to the higher income level and federal government phase out of itemized deductions, 8% is reduced by 40% or 3.2% and the individual nets 4.8% which could then be given to the charity and net affect 40% less income to the charity. Why do we not talk about these methods in everyday conversations? Sounds like the golf course conversation of enlightened advisors!

Chapter

LEASE
EQUIPMENT
BACK
TO
YOUR
COMPANY

LEASE EQUIPMENT BACK TO YOUR COMPANY

There is one technique we have seen utilized with capital-intensive companies such as printers, manufacturing, recycling, or even some service companies like maintenance landscaping. For illustration purposes, we will call the main company ABC LLC. ABC LLC segregates its fixed asset equipment into a new corporation through non-taxable reorganization. We will call it RENTME and ABC LLC will still hold all assets and any licenses necessary for the operation of the business. Next, the ABC LLC will distribute stock of RENTME to the key business owner(s) of ABC LLC. After this occurs, RENTME will operate as an equipment leasing and management company. RENTME will likely elect to be taxed as an S Corporation filing Form 2553. As a leasing company the profits of ABC LLC could be structured to transfer a majority of profits and take advantage of Graduated Tax Rate Planning. In some states there will be a deferred sales taxes over the life of the lease and as a management company RENTME will charge management fees to ABC LLC. Next, all the future fixed assets purchases should likely be done in RENTME. ABC LLC should then elect to be taxed as a C Corporation and file with the IRS. ABC LLC should elect to use a common Paymaster to prevent employees of both organizations from getting higher taxes on FICA, Medicare and unemployment taxes.

What would Graduated Tax Rate Planning provide and why go through this structure? Having the C Corporation serve as the operating company, the first

$50,000 of taxable income would be taxed at 15% federal rate and this would be considerably less than the 28% of S corporation election. What might this provide in real dollars? Varies and it could be zero or it could be $4,000 a year: another great reason to review these issues with a team of advisors.

What will $4,000 earning 8% look like over the next 20 years, funded future medical tax-free? Well it would be an extra $200,000 tax-free, funding lifestyle needs. It all adds up. A little here and a little there makes a huge impact.

What are some reasons companies utilize leasing equipment rather than purchasing? To hold on to capital with little money down. Less financial documentation for lease than loan, opportunity to work capital to add employees or expand into other markets and leases do not impact your balance sheet. We have interviewed several larger company CFOs and the greatest response was no negative impact on balance sheet. It's worth paying 15% interest rate when the capital is freed up and working harder and not showing up as liability as a traditional debt would impact the balance sheet, at least if your company is a publicly traded company. Smaller businesses maybe should not take the idea of leasing the phone and copier equipment. If the finance rate is high, then please have it reviewed by your accountant, legal transaction person or independent leasing specialist. The latter is difficult to find and can be a real plus if you are trying to re-negotiate a lease or purchase out the equipment at the end of the lease. Within the asset protection planning, the norm is setting up separate companies with LLC. Leasing because of the nature of the investments often creates high cash flow and very little in the way of taxes to the investors in leasing ventures. Depreciation and the accelerated schedule allows for many leasing programs to create 100% offset cash flows, thus greater cash flow after tax than most investments. Where would a highly taxed business owner implement a high cash flow vehicle? One place would be where there are significant real estate passive losses that require passive income also known as K-1 income. Ask your accountant about opportunity to match up "passive activity losses" to "passive income generator".

Chapter

WORLD OF ACCREDITED INVESTMENTS

In a 2007 Spectrem Group survey of affluent investors, a whopping 70% of the respondents said their advisors had not even talked to them about alternative investments. The survey went on to reveal an interesting statistic: 33% of the affluent investors said that they were not investing in alternative investments because they perceived them to be "too risky" and 36% said they did not fully understand these investments. There are investments available only to the "accredited investor." The SEC definition of an accredited investor came from the 1940 Investment Act.

Accredited Investor
"A term used by the Securities and Exchange Commission (SEC) under Regulation D to refer to investors who are financially sophisticated and have a reduced need for the protection provided by certain government filings. Also known as *qualified purchaser*."

In order for an individual to qualify as an accredited investor, he or she must accomplish at least one of the following:

1) Earn an individual income of more than $200,000 per year, or a joint income of $300,000, in each of the last two years and expect to reasonably maintain the same level of income.

2) Have a net worth exceeding $1 million, either individually or jointly with his or her spouse.

3) Be a general partner, executive officer, director or a related combination thereof for the issuer of a security being offered.

4) Or, if a trust or corporation, then assets of at least $5 million not necessarily net worth.

These investors are considered to be fully functional without all the restrictions of the SEC.

The premise is that having assets and a higher income level, one is more likely to be financially savvy.

Investments not available to the masses include and are not limited to the following: Performance Fee Money Managers, Exploratory Oil and Gas Drilling, Mineral and other mining operations, royalty, Tenant in Common real estate exchange, private leasing partnerships, Secured Mortgage Notes or Deed Trust Investing, private real estate partnerships, and private money managers with unique asset classes like distressed businesses or credit swaps or hedge funds. We will explore these often-misunderstood investments we will call "alternative" assets. The nice features and sometimes problems of alternative investments have low to zero correlation to the equity markets.

Why are more advisors not tuned into the "Alternative" investments? Some from a lack of license (requires either S 22 or S 7 license). More are a result of compliance officers and back offices not comfortable with offering advanced concept products by neophyte representatives. These alternative products are often difficult to explain and learn and many reps avoid them as a rule.

Why not just run with the masses and jump on mutual fund managers or the heavy marketing gurus touting superior stock selection? Would you prefer to give the government more in the way of short-term capital gains, or have an option to reduce most of these to deferred gains or at least long-term capital gains?

There are many books on advanced subjects usually written to educate the advisor, or the author spelling out all the tax codes as if a business owner is going to be impressed by quoting tax code. We are compelled to make it simple and not overdo the explanations and illustrations.

The masses of America are trusting mutual funds as the main investment vehicle to manage investments and grow money in the equity markets. The masses of America are not "accredited investors" or else they do not understand what is available. Few advisors are willing to invest the time and energy to understand and bring these unique opportunities/investments to you, the Man of Means.

Beware of the hype of some private managers. Let us explain a few ways that these organizations misconstrue the historical performance. One way would be the hypothetical returns based only on a factor such as a specific strategy like "Dogs of Dow" and yet they have not factored in fees and other costs. Another way that results could vary widely, would be when a manager has a basic allocation model or pick of stocks, and the history allows for the results to be a rear looking best-case scenario. These are true only as observations, opinions, and conversations with individuals taken in by hype. Another way is when a strategy uses an index or a blended index and not the actual investments held. Some hypothetical models are picking the lowest day of the month to purchase, looking backwards with picture-perfect vision. Under such a hypothetical, I have seen historical returns in triple digits for the period 2003-2006. Wow! Very impressive. However, if the same indexes and investments were purchased on a consistent basis, like the 15th of each month, then returns are chopped to just a fraction of the perfect and unrealistic view.

There has been a trend over the past 20 years, and even more so lately, that individual investors looking to financial advisors are looking for more than placing their money with great money managers. More and more people look for clear understanding about risks associated with investments and steering clear of pitfalls and tax issues through some level of planning or at the least open communications about "look after me well." Beyond being appreciated as a human being, but knowing that someone is looking out for your best interests. While many advisors are getting some level of training to help identify other concerns and issues, such as estate planning problems developing, they are often not trained on the subtle details to open the communication channels without guiding prospects down a path towards a product sale or gather the assets no matter what.

What are the take-aways from alternative investments? Alternatives are generally tax savvy, allowing individuals with depreciation, credits, passive and active losses to offset in a more efficient fashion. We ask, why lend the government your hard-earned money? That is essentially what occurs when you fail to capture a loss and use it up now.

One tax efficient method of investing is that of buying individual stocks for your time horizon. The problem here is transaction costs and risks in picking a few stocks and not being on top of them 24/7. One way to reduce the individual risks would be to buy a basket of stocks in the form of index or formula investing. We call this method "formulaic investing". Here how this works:

Rationale of Weighting by Fundamentals Versus Other Methods of Index Weighting

The traditional method of capitalization-weighting indices systematically overweights overvalued stocks and underweights undervalued stocks, assuming any price inefficiency. Since investors cannot observe the true fair value of a company, they cannot remove inefficiency altogether but can remove the systematic inefficiency that is inherent in capitalization-weighted indices. Equal-weighting is one method to remove this systematic inefficiency but suffers from high turnover, high volatility, and the requirement to invest potentially large sums in illiquid stocks. Weighting by fundamental factors avoids the pitfalls of equal weighting while still removing the systematic inefficiency of capitalization weighting. It weights industries by fundamental factors (also called "Main Street" factors) such as sales, book value, dividends, earnings, or employees. If a stock's price gets either too high or too low relative to its fair value, weighting by fundamentals will not reflect this bias. This prevents fundamentally based indices from participating in bubbles and crashes and thus reduces its volatility while delivering a higher return. — Wikipedia

ETFs

Professionals interested in finding the most tax efficient investment options available should strongly consider Exchange Traded Funds, or ETFs, as they're more commonly known. These are not only for the accredited investor, but are available to everyone with brokerage accounts. ETFs are one of the fastest growing investment products in the current global financial marketplace. As of January 2007, there are 387 ETFs listed in the U.S. alone, with $422 billion in assets under management. The ETF based on the NASDAQ 100 Index is the number one traded equity security in the world.

ETFs are funds that trade like individual stocks on all of the major exchanges, similar to securities of publicly held companies. They can be bought and sold at any moment during market hours. Of course, they carry the risks involved with traditional investing in stocks, including the possible loss of money. The investment return and principal value of an investment in ETFs will fluctuate so that shares, when sold, may be worth more or less than their original cost.

The Tax-Advantage Design

Taxes are the most overlooked and critical factor in the creation of wealth over time. The unique structure of an ETF allows it to substantially mitigate and or possibly avoid capital gains distributions through an in-kind redemption process. Shareholders may be able to defer some, most or possibly all capital gains until they sell their shares. Not all ETFs have this feature. One story we use to best illustrate this is riding the bus. When you ride the city bus or school bus vs. private transportation, you have to wait for others getting on and off the bus. Each time that bus stops, it is costing you time and money. That is exactly what happens with traditional mutual fund investing.

One way this tax efficiency is accomplished is through a LI–FO (Lowest In – First Out) in-kind tax management strategy. This method typically allows the fund manager, during the creation and redemption process, to purge the lowest cost stocks through in-kind, non-taxable stock transfers. This unique operational trait leaves the fund with the highest cost basis securities, which *systematically reduces tax exposure.*

Mutual Funds, using Highest In – First Out pooled tax treatment strategy for managing most portfolios, typically *creates embedded, unrealized capital-gain exposure* and eventual taxable distributions. These distributions are declared and distributed annually and can occur regardless of whether the investor has made or lost money in the fund. This is like you fell asleep on the bus mentioned above and the driver decided to run a few personal errands in addition to the regular stops.

Separately Managed Accounts (SMAs) allow for customized tax planning and properly align a stock to each individual account, which is a great benefit to wealthy investors. However, when adjusting their portfolios, SMAs *lack an in-kind mechanism by which to purge embedded portfolio gains.*

Finally, ETFs are tax efficient because they trade on an exchange— just like a stock where sellers are matched with buyers. These types of transactions between buyers and sellers do not require the fund to sell stock to meet redemptions. This substantially reduces fund expenses, cash on hand, and the risk of unwanted capital gain distributions.

If your financial advisor is pushing you towards mutual funds or separately managed accounts, you should know that it may be in your best interest tax-wise to ask more questions. If your advisor gets defensive with your questions or starts off defending how your program is better than the S&P 500, then take that as a red flag of ignorance in planning for your tax efficient growth. Most advisors are either afraid of embracing ETFs, or they don't mind what you buy in their wrap fee account, because they make money even if you don't. Finding an advisor that understands and knows how to utilize these very unique investments takes real effort on the part of an advisor or a firm to turn its back on manufactured products.

Efficient Long-Term Investing

According to industry studies over the past few decades, the indexes or benchmarks beat the 80+% of all the funds. At this point, you might come to the conclusion I advocate buying a few well-done indexes and let it be. If the only factor was long-term results and ignoring risks, then yes. Today, the mutual fund industry and the annuity industry have the biggest lobby and budgets for advertising. And according to personalfund.com, expect up to 1% costs for the turnover.

What would an extra 1% return mean over a 20-year period of time? $250,000 invested with 10% vs. 9% would yield an extra $349,731.

Why Mutual Funds and Managed Money may be less efficient

Recently ETFs have been in the news as part of negative reports saying hedge funds and institutional investors have been utilizing ETFs, and some of the major market swings were caused by the limit orders and short selling allowed in ETFs. I found this news not disturbing, but rather flattering, as Institutional Investors are thought to be the most savvy investors of them all, and they discovered not only that ETFs are efficient for tax planning, but efficient for entering and exiting the market with a strategies that work and look very promising for the future. Mutual fund managers mark the end of the day market with *no exit plan.*

Imagine for a minute you have a financial requirement coming up in eight or 10 years and your broker suggests you buy a bond mutual fund. In eight years, the manager is still buying and selling for a pool of money, not for your specific needs. There is no exit strategy with a bond fund or a stock fund. Lining up investments specific to your needs and expectations in the financial industry is nearly impossible due to advisors trying to please management and wholesalers.

Why not use the target date portfolios being touted by many of the largest mutual fund companies? This strategy may in fact work. However, look over the make-up of the portfolio and see if the allocation when adjusted, changes rapidly towards nearly all cash, or cash and bonds with very little stocks, as you approach the target date. This would be like saying you need very little inflation protection at the time you target as the end, and for that matter maybe for the five to 10 years prior to the targeted date. This could be illustrated as: you are riding a long distance bus, and every little town has a stop along the way, thus delaying your arrival at the final destination. There may in fact be a lot of retirees with too little in their target retirement buckets as a result of this continual stop and start process in accommodating all the others on the bus.

In summary, ETFs can be tax efficient, lower cost, liquid, transparent, offer convenient access in and out, and broad diversification. When utilized within a sensible plan, your odds to control risks and get expected results are more likely than getting on a bus and stopping at a lot of other destinations.

Top Money Manager?

Don't fall prey to the idea that some big money manager is going to pay special attention to you and your specific issues. Do not expect a money manager that has attracted billions of dollars to actually have superior results or superior methods to derive exceptional results over a long period of time. What has proven to be the case time after time is this: Select mangers do perform for a period by hedging a substantial position of a winning asset class. Case in point, the

Janus Funds in the late '90s was buying essentially the same stocks as was Fidelity in most of the equity portfolios and was weighted heavily in technology. Janus in 2000 and 2001 was so heavy on outflows from their funds, that managers had to sell when down in the market and this caused more losses and issues. Beware of the marketers touting "beware of the 9 dirty secrets your broker will not share with you." Beware of big marketing firms that mail lots of big packages, and host fancy hotel meetings, and fly in important financial people to tout a performance anomaly.

Ask yourself, are these people really trying to gather my assets without a proper relationship and only to plug one product offering? What do they know about my tax planning needs such as; selling the company in the next few years, and ways to increase your assets through proper planning by 20-50% without taking any stock market risk? We have heard wild things like a revocable trust will help you with asset protection. Obviously, this is not an enlightened advisor. Yes, there are lots of beautiful and friendly people out there with impressive company names backing them, without regards to understanding you and the best possible solutions. Would you expect the hot dog vendor on the street to direct you to the nearest hamburger stand? What do they know about how your estate and legacy is to be conveyed and implemented to your heirs? Could it be that annuities can solve all the financial worries of this world? Some vendor would sure like for you to believe that story. Would it make sense to place all your money in stocks and ride the wave, without a risk managed way to control the downside, be it active management, or put options, or alternative asset classes including defensive bonds? Chances are if you still are reading this book, you have experienced a few of these brokers or agents, and would like to get a handle on how to fix your current investments from the fluctuations of the past and the pain associated. If you keep doing the same thing you will likely get the same results or worse.

Royalty Interest
What are oil and gas mineral, royalty and overriding royalty interests?

Minerals, royalties and overriding royalties receive revenues from the production of oil and gas from a well without paying the drilling or monthly operating expenses from the well.

The term "royalties" can be used interchangeably to mean mineral interests, royalty interests, or overriding royalty interests. However, there is a difference between minerals and royalties, and an even greater difference between overriding royalties and both minerals and royalties. The similarity between mineral interests and royalty interests is that both involve ownership of minerals under the ground. Both receive portions of the income from the production of oil and gas. However, the difference is that the owner of a mineral interest also has the right to execute leases as well as collect bonus payments; whereas, the owner of royalty interests does not execute leases or collect bonus payments.

Diversification is possible with a tax deferral in the form of 1031 exchanges mentioned in the next chapter. Here is the idea. A big investor has a big run up in the real estate market, and wants some diversification of assets. Come to find out after talking with an enlightened advisor, that royalties can qualify for real estate exchange. Royalties may encompass owning leasing and mineral rights on 50,000 or 100,000 wells producing steady income. Now, real estate, instead of producing rents based on the market of commercial real estate, is diversified to allow energy to drive the income source. It's important to have size, capacity, research, relationships and financial strength to get the right leases and be brought the opportunities as a leader in royalty management.

Case for an exchange: Jane buys an office for $200,000 in 1990 and it is valued today at $700,000 and she has a contract to sell. Jane's advisor provides her with a contact for "qualified intermediary or QI" and closing escrowed to QI and then purchases a qualifying royalty set up.

Warrant Income
Investopedia Says:
"The main difference between warrants and call options is that warrants are issued and guaranteed by the company, whereas options are exchange instruments and are not issued by the company. Also, the lifetime of a warrant is often measured in years, while the lifetime of a typical option is measured in months."
We would like to mention only the "Put Warrant" at this time. "Put Warrants" are utilized in stocks and real estate and represent issues directly from a company. A "put option" is similar but not offered from the company, rather a secondary market.

A put warrant represents a certain amount of equity that can be sold back to the issuer at a specified price, on or before a stated date.

Investing In Warrants
Warrants are transferable, quoted certificates, and they tend to be more attractive for medium-term to long-term investment schemes. Tending to be high risk, high return investment tools that remain largely unexploited in investment strategies, warrants are also an attractive option for speculators and are hedges when using both puts and calls. There are also medium risk hard asset warrants with some real backing, not just a potential future business value. We like the hard asset types over the pure stock position every time in terms of the risks. Transparency is high and warrants offer a viable option for private investors as well. This is because the cost of a warrant is commonly low, and the initial investment needed to command a large amount of equity is actually quite small.

With a Put Warrant you are putting a strike price back to the issuer and receiving income which may be taxed or tax deferred and it is possible to pay a capital gains tax rate in the future. Sounds attractive to get a cash flow today and next year and then put the strike price and shares back on the company.

Investing In Preferred Stocks

Big advantage here is the "qualified dividend." Qualified dividends are taxed at 15% capital gains rates rather than ordinary income rates of many investments. Looking at high yielding corporate bond, perhaps 7% and 7% Preferred Stock, the tax structure would in fact be different. Bonds are taxed as ordinary income at 35% federal and the preferred would be taxed at 15% capital gains rate. Paying 20% more taxes can add up over time. Caution, many of these have recently priced themselves to be only a little better than ordinary dividend and income investments!

Secured notes or Deed Trust Financing

A deed of trust, also known as a trust deed, is a unique form of loan recorded within public records as a deed that has a lien on the property. Trust deeds are used by borrowers instead of conventional mortgages. This is usually done in order to obtain greater flexibility on the loan that would be available under the rules and regulations in standard lending institutions such as banks. Also could be called collateralized or secured mortgages.

There are three main parties involved. These parties include the trustor - which is the person who is borrowing the money - the beneficiary - also known as the lender - as well as a neutral third party. This third party is the trustee, who temporarily holds part of the property title until the loan is paid in full.

Once the entire obligation has been met by the trustor, then the deed of trust is considered cancelled. Until that time, the trustee holds the ability to foreclose on the property if the obligations are not met by the trustor. This can be done without ever having to use the court system, and is therefore a much faster and more direct foreclosure than would occur in the case of a typical mortgage.

Therefore, as you can see, trust deeds are quite the secure form of investment for many people. Since the collateral on the loan is the property itself, which usually has a greater value than the loan itself, it means that there is a great deal of security offered on the loan. For this reason, trust deed investing is becoming increasingly popular in a great many states among people who are seeking low-risk investments with high returns. This idea of secured in first position and having control to foreclose, has unique advantages over many over investments such as stock, bonds and mutual funds not secured and controlled.

Sometimes you will hear people talk about this being a "hard asset" in the fact that there are hard assets backing the paper. Most of the time it is investors buying what is called fractional shares or units in LLC or Partnership. Most people do not have millions of dollars to set up a direct secured note so they buy into a more simple approach in the fractional shares.

Risk

What are the main types of risk?

1. Foreclosure
2. Delayed Payment of Interest
3. Defective Title
4. Disasters
5. Current Taxes
6. Incorrect Appraisal
7. Improper Recording of Trust Deed
8. Position of Loan
9. Hidden Liens (e.g. Mechanical Lien)
10. Construction Issues

We believe proper due diligence is the best place to start. Have your advisors ask lots of questions and get third party review when feasible.

Private Investment Partnerships provide a different structure in which to operate "the partnership." The power of matching up passive income to passive losses should not be overlooked. (Passive Income Generator a.k.a. "PIG"). Passive Activity Loss or "PAL" when matched up with PIG makes for a high level of income tax advantaged. A common example: Investor buys real estate cash generator, and also buys loss activity with in a tax credit or oil and gas drilling partnership.

K-1 distributions are basically mini-investment companies. Not all private investments are K-1 in nature. Some are structured as an LLC with either S or C Corporation election.

One of my favorite alternative investments, leaning towards a more conservative investor yet with strong performance, would be a secured note or senior mortgage notes or also called deed trust investing. Investors like the idea of not locking up money. Longer term and short-term notes in the 30 day to 18 month range, fits well with many looking for returns greater than corporate bond markets, with less risk of default or at least the funds would be secured. Investors like knowing there is backing or collateral on their money. Low loan to value ratios, strong asset review process, third party appraisals and people that have stood the test of bumpy credit and real estate markets make good business partners. We like seeing due diligence reports from industry experts regarding such investments as well. Historically we have seen significant returns greater than the Lehman Brothers Corporate Bond Index. Larger investors like to know there is an exit and process to capture returns few are willing to work to create. These are not mutual funds nor are they hedge funds. Why are these investments only available in a private memorandum? The costs to roll out marketing materials and getting publicly registered investments is cost prohibitive for the size of many real estate deals as well as other offerings. Time is another important factor restricting many of these to investment management and development companies. Some work in a narrow niche and will never get into the mainstream of investments. Some are too complicated for normal public disclosure according to the vendors or suppliers we have talked with over the years.

Performance Fee or Incentive Fee Money Management

We see lots of people use the term performance fee when what they are describing is really a fulcrum fee or sliding scale fee structure. Many of the larger mutual fund companies have incentives for the manager to outperform their measuring benchmark. Hedge funds have performance or incentive fees as well. Some are very steep, maybe 10-30% of the gains above a measuring index. We found several research articles on Google search and from www.cepr.org (Center for Economic Policy Research). Some incentive fee managers take on too much risk, according to some articles we researched. Several articles go on to state that without accountability and risk management the investor may be in big beta or risk fluctuations. As a money manager you get paid according to the results you produce. Everyone loves to talk about performance and very few mention risk, it seems. The sliding scale or fulcrum fee looks like this: the mutual fund manager that produces more than the measuring benchmark, like the S&P 500, will make more fees, and if under performing, then a much lower fee. We have seen fees range a tremendous amount, and as an investor, many would be willing to pay more for more results. One group that started doing this over a longer period of time, four years rolling average, has risk measures put into place to hold managers accountable. It is one of the five largest mutual fund companies. They started this process in the late 1950s and it still holds true today due to the risk management, in our opinion.

Hedge funds and private money managers have utilized this method to place their money where their mouth is. They place in writing "no fees if under perform the benchmark and a percentage of the amount above the benchmark." How does an individual investor hold the manager accountable for the risks taken? Are the incentives on the up side so great that the downside is overlooked in the manager's eyes? Then who bears the risks? The investor, of course, bears that risk.

An example of this may be; Joe buys $250,000 into a private money manager that states the benchmark is the EAFE World Index and the funds out perform over the next year by 5% gross. The manager gets 1% if at or below the benchmark, and then gets 20% of the excess over the benchmark, or in this example another 1% for a total of 2%. Another case may be, if out performing the benchmark by 2%, then take 20% of the total return, so 20% return and benchmark was, say, 15%, then the manager fee would be 4% and maybe zero if performing at or below the benchmark.

We are not saying that incentive or performance fees are good or bad. It's another way to look at the way you pay for money management. If your waiter at a restaurant is rude and mean vs. prompt and friendly, are you tipping the same way? If you list your home with a professional realtor and they are not able to sell it, do you still pay them? When they do sell it they get paid rather well, would you agree? Many attorneys and sales people work on a contingency basis: If they help you, then they are rewarded and if not, then they are not compensated. It's about how you want to pay for services. It's been our experience that people are intrigued and interested to talk about performance fee or incentive fee money management. It does make sense to pay for performance and pay less or almost nothing for lack of performance. The papers on the internet looking into the Hedge Fund sector that have performance fees, seem to conclude that one generally takes on more risks in order to perform, and thus earn the managers and investors greater returns. We believe this can work well with proper risk structure, both active measures and passive methods combined, the passive method utilizing the proper allocation and diversification into several asset buckets. The active being utilizing "put options" and active measures such as outside review of manager risk and their models on a regular basis.

Not only hedge funds and private equity managers utilize this strategy, but the real estate sector has utilized these incentives for decades. These usually take on a look of return of principal, then specified rate of return in simple interest terms, then a sharing arrangement above that amount. For example: Joe buys $100,000 into a real estate partnership. The sharing fee arrangement may state once the principal is returned, then a simple annual interest of 8% per year, and then a sharing arrangement of 80/20 investor to money manager. So, Joe gets $100,000 plus five years of 8% simple interest or another $40,000 and then sharing kicks in, and if sold for $200,000, then the $60,000 above the $140,000 is split. Joe gets another $48,000 and the manager gets $12,000 incentive or sharing. An excellent web site to find out more about alternative investments is www.caia.org then click on Alternative Investments and then look up articles. This is the site for the Chartered Alternative Investment Analyst Association or CAIA.

Oil and Gas Exploration and Developmental Drilling
In 1967, Congress enacted a little known provision in the Tax Code, known as "Intangible Drilling Costs", also known as IDC deduction. This was implemented to encourage domestic oil and gas exploration for "homeland security," not relying on other countries for our oil supply. These IDCs are anything but intangible. They are easy to count and account for in real terms with significant tax benefits. Do not buy these just for the tax benefits. The programs you consider should stand on their own regardless of tax reduction benefits. Intangible Drilling Costs deductions are subject to Alternative Minimum Tax reductions and some are taken upfront, and others are spread over a two or three year period. They differ based on the sponsors set up and the processes utilized in drilling. Exploration has little to no IDC until actual drill and work to bring into production is completed.

Developmental drilling is what many refer to as poking holes in the ground and hooking it up to a pipeline. Often shallow wells are easier to drill with moderate to low flow rates and many last for several years. We have visited wells like this over 50 years old and still producing. The probability of hitting oil or gas in this type of setting is usually very high with little risk on the downside other than energy price and lower than expected rates of flow. It would be very rare to have a super high output well in these developmental drills unless higher risk deep drilling is done with higher pressures associated with the deeper drills.

Exploration Drilling has higher risk, higher return potential. There are some new tools just out in the past few years that have increased the accuracy of drilling and new bit designs, equipment, and materials for drilling in all directions. Finding the oil or the "prospects" of oil starts with geologist, seismic, or 3D seismic studies. Partnering with the right people is key in the oil business even more so than other industries in our opinion.

Real Estate Partnerships

This is one area that demands special attention to the type of advisor you work with regarding these varied programs. The spectrum of real estate ranges from early stage land banking, to land banking with entitlements being secured, to opportunity for early development, to buy and hold and buy, to exit and reclamation, and older property service programs. Obviously there are other fits like Timberland, Unique Real Estate Situations, Special Notes with Purchase options etc.

While we address the broad categories here, realize that getting a fit for your objectives and also having a due diligence on the providing organization is critical for your future chances of real success.

Early Stage Land Banking: no income and all potential capital gains

Latter Stage Land Banking: some income, preferred, warrants, accrual plus capital gains.

Development or Opportunity: usually taking raw entitled land and turning out a project for capital appreciation with little regards to income.

Mature or Developed Properties: looking for a way to bring value to existing properties in the form of better management, and marketing or changing the targeted end user.

Reclaim or Rehab Marketplace: usually involves redevelopment or gut out construction, or again, taking an aging property and breathing new life into it with new capital and/or positioning. Great examples might include old movie houses turning into community churches, or an old downtown YMCA into student housing.

Again, real estate is a unique asset in the fact that borrowing money efficiently is a key factor in leveraging up the returns. Real estate is, and will continue to be, both a wealth builder and income provider, depending on the market sector and stage of investment that fits your needs or agenda.

Chapter

BUYING
LIFE
INSURANCE

BUYING LIFE INSURANCE

If your business is a C Corporation, then a "Section 79" Plan may fit the ticket for employees to purchase life insurance on a pre-tax funded basis. If properly structured to have a Life Insurance Trust own the policy, then the entire proceeds could pass both income and estate tax free to your heirs. The plan may not discriminate in favoring key employees and the employer may not be directly or indirectly the beneficiary of the plan. In other words, this is not a plan to fund key man life insurance on a pre-tax basis.

The practicable application here is for an employer to offer to purchase a $50,000 policy on all the employees. Of course, the rank and file will opt out due to the taxable nature to employees. They will choose not to be taxed on the economic benefit. What would this look like for you as employer?

You're a small employer with a Defined Benefit Plan and you wish to purchase life insurance with pre-tax dollars. Placing the proper kind of life insurance policy inside your plan can also greatly increase the amount of dollars to fund the benefits. If the objective is to get as bigger tax deduction, then utilization of guaranteed whole life would best fit the bill. Many advisors and accountants are dogmatic about not to ever use guaranteed whole life. Here may be an area to relax, or at the least, reconsider the position. Maybe your plan is considered over funded (the accumulated and funded dollars exceed the actuarial need by 50%?) If this is the case, then a common strategy would be to purchase a cash value life policy with lots of guarantees and then consider taking a distribution of the policy and paying the taxes and/or costs to get dollars out of your plan. Tell a professional agent with lots of resources behind him to get back with you promptly. If they tell you it will be a week or two before they can get with you in this area, then it might just be a red flag that they are not on top of this, and do not have ready access to the players in this arena. Buying a life policy is better than getting penalized by the government for serious over-funding at a 50% tax rate. See, the IRS Game is just that. When you fund it too much, then the IRS takes one-half away, and if you don't take out enough after age 70 ½, then there is also a 50% penalty for not paying taxes on time per the IRS schedule. If you want more retirement income, for the same dollars contributed, you may want to include life insurance for its unique income tax benefits. If you decided that you will not spend your last dollar on your last day here on earth then consider placing life insurance inside your plan. Here is just another good reason to have a team of advisors looking out for you.

Another efficient way to buy permanent coverage is to purchase life insurance inside the private captive insurance company. Warning here: You need to be very clear about your objectives in captive planning. There is a place where buying life insurance inside the captive is not a good idea at all. See the Captives and Retirement Plan chapters for the pros and cons of each of these plans.

Private Placement Life Insurance: How is it different than buying regular life insurance off the shelf? If an offshore location is utilized, then often we see very flexible investment opportunities not available inside the domestic boxes. One example is "Guaranteed Insurance Contracts", or GICS as they are known, as one type of fixed investment. Without layers of commissions, and legal and state regulators' costs, these historically have produced in the last decade an 8% fixed rate. Another example is: you have a private money manager running stocks or other holdings for you and they could be a sub account manager for such a policy. Many of the Accredited Investor Programs in the chapter "Accredited Investor" are also available inside your life policy. Very different than the same old mutual fund type investments found in variable life contracts. You could also hold hard assets managed by a friend or a private company stock—not your own, though. Insurance regulations require diversification under Section 817h of the Tax Code. The "prudent man" rule for the types of investments you purchase should always be the norm. You cannot control the private assets such as your private corporation or your own real estate portfolio. Rules are strict here and not to comply will negate the entire program.

This can be a part of your overall wealth strategy and part of your funding private holdings. Private placement variable life insurance is basically the same as regular policies purchased by agents except the investment options have much greater flexibility and are unique choices. These are for accredited investors only.

Private Placement policies have been abused in the past and are potentially subject to a series of revenue rulings issued by the Internal Revenue Service in the late 1970s and early 1980s. They are known as the "investor control" rulings. So if the policyholder has control directly over the investments rather than hiring a manager, then creates a swing towards more control, it will subject the assets held to be taxed on the accumulation inside the policy.

It is not clear when this idea of too much control occurs. Generally, it's important to hire hedge fund managers or established money managers that will not do exactly what you are saying. In fact, they should get a clear idea of what you want to accomplish and work within an Investment Policy Statement for all future transactions. Last of all, many of these policies are expensive and they can be custom designed with lower expenses. Higher up front cost may be fine if the opportunity within the investment area is significant enough. We see some nice note and income investments not available to the general public inserted into these policies and without market risk.

Buying Term Life Insurance is a consideration. First, if you are in a high-risk occupation or have very high-risk hobbies, then please purchase the waiver of premium coverage. This is the provision that kicks in if you become disabled and pays the premiums. Ask your agent if it pays for lifetime or if only to age 65. Next, consider the return of premium provision especially if you are buying, say, a 30-year level premium term policy. What is return of premium? You pay a premium that is a little higher than level premium and, if you do not die, then at the end of the period you get all the premiums back. Depending on what stats you read, the insurance companies expect that 93% of the term policies will lapse without paying anything. It's not a waste if you pay $800 a year for $1 million of coverage for 20 years and you get to the end and you are not dead. You had peace of mind knowing the coverage was in place for your family or other commitments.

Another important aspect of buying a term policy is getting one with a conversion option and understanding what that means. It is the right of the client to convert the term policy, without medical questions, to a permanent plan. Examples of permanent plans would include whole life, variable life, universal life, and the cash value accumulation types of policies. This is vital if one suffers from a prolonged illness where one would not be able to obtain coverage. Many term policies have a limited amount of time like five or 10 years of a 20-year policy. Another great reason to ask your enlightened advisor about what other types of policies this could convert into in the future.

If you missed the IRA Maximization section in Retirement Plans, then go back and read it.

What about selling your policy or your parents' life insurance policy? There is a whole market out there driven by large institutions to fund the buyout of policies provided the insured is over age 65 and even better if there is a change of health or change of circumstances.

One friend of mine explains his service this way. Senior settlement broker is a resource for advisors with client's considering 1035 exchanges, surrendering policy for cash value or lapsing a policy. Broker's work with policies no longer needed or wanted for estate and business planning clients. He does not originate life policies for re-sale. Most of his clients use proceeds to fund new policies or other investments. The term used to describe this marketplace is called "Life Settlements or Senior Settlements." The insured are expected to live greater than 24 months and it was born out of the viatical settlement market. Viaticals are for individual insureds under age 65 and expected to live less than 24 months. The senior or life settlement market was born out of the viatical market and became very viable when large financial institutions started funding or ceded these transactions. The media created some stink about viatical transactions, creating a lot of bad will in the industry based on individuals profiting from other's mortality. Your enlightened advisor ought to have access and firsthand knowledge of the people in this unique industry. There may be gold in those old policies. Oh, by the way, many companies will not talk to you unless the policy face amount is over $100,000. Your enlightened advisor should direct you to a brokerage of life settlements rather than one company. Reasons: shopping the market, sending only to those companies willing to consider, reducing time in the process. What could you expect from a quality life settlement broker? When would someone wish to sell a policy? They have no need for coverage or rather than simply cash it in for the stated cash value. Shop it to see if a better offer may be had. If the insured is over age 70, many of these policies are worth more than the amount the insurance carriers list as surrender value. Another reason for selling a policy would be inability to make the current premiums. Ask your enlightened advisors about shopping the market and find out what is the current market. You may be quite pleased. There is a resource to consider looking over for guidelines and rules in the life settlement market. Go to www.lisassociation.org for the life insurance settlement association web site.

Chapter

10

REAL
ESTATE
EXCHANGES

REAL ESTATE EXCHANGES

A real estate exchange is a method to transfer the gains without taxation to the new property. For the purposes of this discussion we will address only IRC Section 1031. Why, How, When?

Let me tell you a story about three real estate investors, Tom, Dick and Harriett.

Tom, Dick and Harriett all received an equal share in some land and a warehouse as an inheritance 20 years ago from their parents' estate. The property was valued at $300,000 at that time so each share was worth $100,000. Last month, they received an offer and decided to sell it for $3 million after all expenses. Each of them now has $1 million net after all costs. So they all will make the same money, right? Well, not really.

Let's talk about Tom first. Tom doesn't like to try new things. (He still believes that Windows 95 is the best operating software for his 10-year-old computer!) Tom decided to just pay the taxes on the gain and, unfortunately for him, did not seek any outside advice on this. So this is what his deal looks like: $100,000 original value deducted from the $1 million sale price nets him $900,000. His gain is taxed at 15% (or $135,000). Next, remember that the original $100,000 was depreciated over the last 20 years (he did have a decent accountant) so this portion was taxed at 25% or another $25,000 out of his pocket. That brought his total net down to $840,000.

Tom took his money and bought some bonds and CDs. His overall returns will be about 6% on the

$840,000 so he will earn approximately $50,400 a year. Not bad, but remember that Tom will get little to no upside appreciation due to the fact that CDs and bonds are not guaranteed to appreciate.

Next, let's look at his brother Dick's approach to the same situation. Dick looks at several options including charitable trusts, deferred exchanges and the installment sale. All of these would allow him to defer (or even potentially avoid) the taxes, or at least spread them out over a longer period of time. Dick now has the use of an additional $160,000 that Tom paid in taxes giving him more equity and working capital in the future. Dick decides to do a deferred exchange. He made sure to have the proper language in the closing documents and he also hired a Qualified Intermediary. For a few hundred dollars, he now has control over when he pays taxes.

So let's look at what is happening here: He sells today without taxes and places the money into another property. After careful consideration, Dick decides to do this in a special asset protected vehicle. The full $1 million goes in and Dick was also able to secure another $1 million of non-recourse debt allowing him to buy a $2 million property! The cash flow is much more than his brother Tom's portfolio and he has $2 million working for him to grow in the future.

Let's recap here: Dick sells and buys another property and pays no capital gains taxes and no recapture taxes. All of the money is working for him plus another $1 million he secured for the deal. The potential is great for Dick's family as the $2 million portfolio has twice as much potential for growth.

Lastly, we come to kind and generous Harriett. She is not looking for a large cash windfall. She wants the money to benefit her children and grandchildren. Harriett does not like the idea of paying $160,000 in taxes. She wanted to plan the best way to move money to her children and grandchildren while avoiding estate taxes. She wanted a way to stretch out the capital gains costs over her lifetime, too.

She now has a trust with special provisions to exclude it from her estate and the money is invested without taxation today. She agreed to place the money in the trust, take only a fixed payment from the trust, and the remainder goes to the family, potentially escaping both estate and capital gains taxes. She receives monthly cash flow on the entire $1 million and it can be invested and moved to meet her needs in the future.

Picture this: If she dies 10 years later and the family gets it all tax free, WOW! If she were in a high tax bracket, as most people in this type of situation are, then the family would expect to pay 50% of the estate value in taxes. Without this type of planning, it could cost them hundreds of thousands of dollars when they least expected it. Good Job, Harriett.

The story of Tom, Dick and Harriett has a happy ending. Tom did not have to learn anything new and still put money in his pocket, Dick was able to do much more and get a bigger cash flow at the same time, and as for Harriett, well, she was able to do exactly what she wanted for herself and others. In the process of getting cash for herself and locking in a gain in the real estate market, she protected the money while avoiding a significant tax liability.

In their eyes, each was successful. The key was finding someone with the skills to provide them with the solution tailored to meet their specific needs.

Let me ask you five key questions that most people never ask themselves:

1. Does it ever bother you when you're forced to pay taxes today that you could defer for years—or even avoid?

2. Are you the type of person who is open to exploring options that could provide 15 to 20% more cash flow from your next sale or property transfer <u>without any increase in risk</u>?

3. Suppose you found an extra $100,000 today hidden within one of your current investments.

Would you be willing to give most of that to your favorite charity (or the government) when you leave this earth?

4. Do you know if capital gain tax rates are going down, going up, or will remain the same over your lifetime?

5. How will these types of decisions affect your retirement picture?

Dick, the second investor, utilized a 1031 exchange. The rules for the exchange work this way. First, you need to establish a relationship with a Qualified Intermediary. These are escrow agents and can be a great resource. They should be bonded and insured and experienced in the process. Be careful because if you go online or look in the phone book for a "qualified intermediary", then you will likely get an attorney who is a part-time realtor trying to sell you something, or a realtor/mortgage/title person trying to sell their services and a few others' services as well. Next, after selling, you have 45 days from the sales closing to identify the new property or properties and a total of 180 days to close on the new "replacement property." Yes, you can change into more than more property. The 1031 exchanges have been around for over 85 years, and they got a lot easier in 2001, with Congress passing legislation allowing for The Tenet In Common method and the Delaware Statutory Trust to make the process for finding replacement properties much easier. Both methods brought the Securities Registered real estate into the picture. Below is a description of Tenant In Common or "TIC" as most refer to it.

The Tenant in Common association describes TIC in the following way:

Tenant-in-Common is a form of holding title to real property. It allows the owner/owners to own an undivided fractional interest in the entire property. In addition, it has become the preferred investment vehicle for real property investors, who wish to defer capital gains via a 1031 exchange and own real property without the management headaches.

A popular choice among real estate investors seeking replacement property for their IRC Section 1031 tax deferred exchange is Tenant-in-Common Ownership (TIC), also known as fractional ownership. Under this co-ownership structure, you will own an undivided fractional interest in an entire property and share in your portion of the net income, tax shelters, and growth. Further, you will receive separate deed and title insurance for your percentage interest in the property, and have the same rights as a single owner. Because TIC opportunities are often "packaged" with management and financing in place, TICs offer superior efficiencies in the identification, acquisition, financing, closing, and operating stages of real estate ownership.

Furthermore, fractional ownership provides you with the ability to diversify your 1031 Tax Free Exchange into more than one property, and to participate in potentially larger, institutional quality properties. Thus, small investors in one area of the country may participate in large industrial, commercial, and residential property investments all around the country with professional management.

TIC investments provide simplicity by eliminating active property management headaches. Individuals who are tired of the day-to-day burdens of being landlords or who own land and would like an income producing property will appreciate the benefits of a TIC investment. The TIC program gives you a "coupon clipper" or "mailbox management" investment that can save you time and money.

• Cash flow is generally paid monthly and is tax-sheltered via depreciation pass through and interest deductions. You may also share in the appreciation of the property when sold.

• Minimum equity requirements as low as $100,000 allow you to invest in high quality, institutional grade properties. Otherwise, it may be prohibitive for you to acquire property with a billion-dollar credit-worthy tenant guaranteeing a long-term lease. These low minimums also allow you to diversify, which can reduce your risk by allowing investments in different locations, with various property types, tenants, industries, etc.

• National real estate companies that structure these TIC programs acquire (identify and locate, evaluate, arrange financing, etc.), manage (maintain, lease, collect rent, service mortgage), and sell the TIC properties. They have a vested interest in the performance of the property. These companies have strong track records, and extensive experience in all sectors, types, and locations of real estate.

• TICs enable you to replace the required debt on the 1031 when needed. Accredited investors assume non-recourse (no personal guarantee) financing existing on the property. You can invest in properties that have no debt or in ones with up to 75% leverage.

• TICs provide the flexibility to avoid the taxable boot if your preferred real estate doesn't allow you to meet the full debt and equity requirements.

• A ready inventory of TIC properties allows individuals to easily identify properties within the 45-day identification period, acquire within the 180 days, or have a "back-up" property in case their preferred real estate falls through.

A Delaware Statutory Trust or "DST" as it's known in the industry works this way:

Do we only look at the tax saved today? No way. It's about the opportunity of paying the taxes today, versus letting the money that would have been paid in taxes, work now for you. According to NACREF (www.nacreaf.org)

the industry average for office properties as a group has amounted to a total annualized return of 9.29% since 1978. Let's assume an investor has savings of $100,000 in taxes and now has the opportunity to work that money for another 20 years. The advantage here would be an additional $636,000+. Understand why this is receiving so much attention in the financial services industry?

The option of "1031 exchange" is taught in the real estate, financial services, and legal fields to be a big opportunity potential for those with products to move. Currently, the financial services field has the advantage of available and well-positioned product offerings in the form of TIC's or DSTs. Realtors are not allowed to offer these products unless they have a securities license as well. Let me state a word of warning here: Just because you can identify a property doesn't mean it will be there for you when you need to close. On the standard 1031 exchange you can identify three properties and we recommend it. Things change, deals fall apart, funding of a TIC sometimes moves really fast. We have seen $50-100 million dollar deals go in a few days, and the smaller deals go in a few hours. We have seen a few deals not move fast for good reasons: low cap rate, only 4% cash flow and high expense with little upside potential. Some of these deals never fund properly, get pulled, and leave the exchanger (you) without the tax swap opportunity. In these cases, however, they can be avoided for the most part. Get an experienced person that represents lots of companies, has a large inventory to work with, knows the downside, and shares that with you up front.

One method real estate investors utilize here is called the "roll till you drop." We have an elderly widow with non-income producing property who wants a current income without paying taxes today. Could be like Dick or Harriett in the story above. So if Dick exchanges into a TIC and later, say seven years from now, the TIC is selling out, then Dick needs to search for another property or properties to continue deferring the capital gains. Under the current estate tax code, when someone dies and leaves property with capital gains, the heirs receive a step-up in basis to the value upon the death of the individual. So Dick has basis originally of $100,000 in the warehouse and it gets depreciated to nothing and then exchanged without taxes and then exchanged again and again for other properties. If these are qualified exchanges, then upon Dick's passing, the inheritance value of, say, $2 million is stepped up and there are no capital gains taxes.

Lastly, very few advisors know how to exchange your investment property or properties into oil and gas royalties. These mineral rights program are written and combine like the TIC and DST. Instead of commercial property, however, like offices, apartments and the like, it's owning part of say thousands or even hundred of thousands of oil and gas wells pumping 24/7 to provide cash flow and further diversification.

What is a DST? A Delaware Statutory Trust is a separate legal entity created as a trust under Delaware statutory law. The law permits a very flexible approach to design and operations of the entities.

The differences:

• The lenders prefer the DST as it will deal only with one entity and make one loan as opposed to 34 borrowers and the paperwork for each of those loans. The TIC format is for a single member limited liability company and each investor would need to be approved.

• DST has very strong asset protection in that if one of the parties declares bankruptcy, the creditors of the beneficiary will not be able to reach the DST asset. With no potential for liens against the asset, the lender is always in first position on the loan and could foreclose in first position.

• Investors are shielded from liabilities, thus no need for a separate limited liability company and lower formation and lower annual costs. It is less complex for investors and no need to address carve outs of non-recourse debt. Last, a DST will allow a beneficiary to do a tax-free exchange of a pro rata share of the DST when it is sold off.

• DST may provide much greater diversification holding several properties.

Currently there was a ruling this week to allow realtors to work with enlightened advisors in offering both TIC and DST structures.

Chapter 11

REAL ESTATE

REAL ESTATE

When you played Monopoly as a child, did you ever win by just passing go and collecting $200? Not likely. If all you did was work and collect a paycheck from an employer then it would difficult to win financially unless you were in a highly specialized niche that paid very well. Owning the Electric Company or Water Works or owning houses and hotels that paid your rent and revenues was the key factor in winning Monopoly. Another observation made about the game was that if the other players all owned the properties, then you just prayed to land on Community Chest, Chance, Free Parking or—even Go to Jail was better! Interesting how childhood games play out in our lives, and congratulations on being the business owner and real estate mogul.

So if you own your own business and have been paying rent, then you need to read this short chapter. If you have been reaping the rewards of owning your business property and wish to expand or downsize, then check out our web site posting some strategies to help you at www.financialfarmer.com.

If you can get a property that is not "Class A," brand new or completely remodeled, then there may be some advantages for you tax wise. If you have to have a very specific type of property such as medical space, manufacturing with specific needs, then you, too, should go to our web site and look for "cost segregation" studies to get more money in your pocket today. Even if you have already purchased a property in the past few years, then you can potentially accelerate your depreciation and put real dollars in your pocket today and over the next couple of years.

Some advantages of owning you might miss in the typical costs analysis may include customizing your space, ease of renting out a portion, how your deal is structured, and the method by which you write off expenses. All of these are decisions you make with or without thought to outcome.

Some say they like the control of picking whom they associate with and who are the tenants. Others love the fact that custom decorations attached to the building are deductible expenses and important for the culture and feel of the office. Another friend enjoys the freedom to see the business cash flow a deductible expense "rent" to personally held property. Others enjoy funding improvements from cash flow and increasing the value of personal assets with business dollars.

Accountants often tell you to own it personally. There are a lot of issues to address (expand on taxation today expected taxation in the future, estate planning issue to transfer to children, if substantial asset may want to consider a Family Limited Partnership, For privacy concerns find the State or method by which held will need to be addressed) as to the way it's held, which will determine future taxes and each method will have a different impact on protecting the real property from liabilities. In Florida the preferred way to hold real estate is the Limited Liability Company or LLC. An LLC can elect how it will be taxed, either as an S-Corp flow through to individual members or as a C-Corp with a C-Corp tiered tax structure. Just because your property is in Florida or California or Texas doesn't mean you need to incorporate your building in that state. Nevada and Delaware are much better choices for not allowing Internet access to ownership information. Land Trusts are another method and they have some advantages in privacy and may, in fact, provide some financial benefits in the future. Again get with your local enlightened advisors as to how this should be held.

Real estate is a unique investment asset in that the cost of leverage to purchase property is relatively cheap in comparison to margin and risk of calls in an investment portfolio. Lending provisions for investment property are highly accessible and at much higher levels than other investments. Question: How much real estate can you buy with $100,000 cash? If you answered $100,000, then you are missing the power of real estate and leverage. It may be that you can purchase $400,000 or up to $1 million in property depending on several factors. Now, how much IBM stock could you buy with $100,000? Without a potentially painful call from your broker, only $100,000. Okay, if you do margin or borrow on the stock you may purchase, let's say, $200,000. This is not to make a comparison of real estate to equities, but rather the powerful impact of leverage in real estate holdings.

Chapter

12

EMPLOYEE STOCK OWNERSHIP PLAN

What is an ESOP or Employee Stock Ownership Plan? First, it's a regulated governmental employee benefit under the Employee Retirement Income Security Act 1974, a.k.a. ERISA. An ESOP allows employees to gain stock in their company without investing their own money. As an owner in a closely held corporation, this sounds twisted and maybe too generous. There are other aspects to ESOP that make this idea attractive when properly applied.

The most common use of ESOP is to buy out a departing stockholder and defer taxes on the ESOP, providing the ESOP is properly funded. ERISA's definition of properly funded would be that 30% of the outstanding stock is held by the ESOP. Oh, and the purchase of the stock was done with pre-tax dollars as well. Sweet.

Another use for ESOP is expansion. Leveraged or borrowed money is used to fund the purchase of stock, then utilize the stock of your company to buy another company and do it all while writing off the interest costs because of the unique nature of the ERISA employee benefit plan. The 401(k) Profit Sharing Plan will not accomplish this on its best day.

If you are looking for a way to fund your own retirement from tax savvy internal sales to employees and pass the baton to them, an ESOP might be the ticket. First, before you get excited there are several steps to consider. Do a feasibility study, hire a consultant, set up a trust document; get a real appraisal, not some general opinion. All of these cost real money and take time and energy to fulfill and keep current year after year. This strategy is a big winner for the right person and the right kind of company that either wants to buy other companies for 65 cents on the dollar or someone who wants a tax efficient method to retire and have the employees own and run the enterprise.

Who sets up these plans? Generally, we have seen companies adopt ESOP that have steady and strong cash flows with 10 or more employees. Many of the Fortune 500 companies have them in place.

Remember, this is an ERISA employee benefit and looks like other ERSIA retirement plans. Include employees that work 1000 hours in a year, and a vesting schedule 20%, 40%, 60%, 80%, 100%, like a 401(k). A Form 5500 must be filed each year. This is a "Qualified Plan" for purposes of tax planning. The key difference in funding the plan is twofold: 1) Fund with closely held stock called a stock bonus plan 2) Borrow funds from a lending institution and deduct interest payments (also called a "Leveraged Plan").

Appraisal Costs? We have seen typical costs of $5,000 to $15,000 for a closely held corporation. Beware, there a few companies out there charging significantly greater amounts. The appraisal should include the following:

- Appraiser's experience and any court testifying experience

- Initial cost to complete, and future schedule of costs

- Cost of repurchase liability study

- Time frame to complete, once supplied with corporate documents

Administration Costs of about $1800 base fee plus $25-$50 per participant are rates quoted to us in the Southeast. Many of the 401(k) Third Party Administrators may also provide ESOPs.

Legal Fees for setting up and running an ESOP are difficult to quote due to potentially lots of moving parts. Plan document set-up fees, repurchase review fees, trustee-required review fees, and maybe individual owner representative legal fees.

The Plan is established as a trust and trustees generally vote, although the employees can be given the power to vote on major issues such as the sale of the company. Often, key officers or directors of the corporation act as trustees. Some plans hire independent trustees or combine outside individuals with key management. Remember, the employees are not the direct shareholders. Rather, the trustees of the ESOP hold company stock.

Previous to the Enron situation, it was common to see large corporations use their company stock when matching employee contributions. Today there seems to be a fear of the government coming in or attorneys coming in and threatening lawsuits. The prudent trustee would now match in cash and allow the employee to choose which investments they want in addition to allowing employees to choose, it would also provide educational materials regarding diversification and risk. Meanwhile, ESOPs are still funded with only company stock.

One incentive for a business owner to fund an ESOP is the following: deductibility of dividends, which is great for cash flow. Dividends are used to either pay debt or reduce principal. There is tax deduction for dividends paid on company stock bought by the ESOP with a loan. There are some taxes to be paid by employees for this ownership privilege.

The last powerful provision ESOP provides is known as the "Section 1042" rollover. The ESOP must own at least 30% after sale and the seller must reinvest the proceeds within twelve months. Then the acquired stock must be held for three months to qualify for the tax deferral on the sale. Currently if the seller held the stock until his death, the heirs or beneficiaries would receive a step up in basis and would not be taxed on all the gains accumulated in the business and subsequent stock gains. Wow! What a powerful way to exit and provide savvy tax planning to your heirs.

The conclusion on an ESOP is that it is a unique and powerful way to either exit your business or expand business with tax savvy dollars. It can be a great incentive tool to get employees to think about saving money and focus on company ownership. It can also be a powerful way to build financial wealth over the long haul. Be sure you don't hear only the good stuff, but hear clearly that debts and the interest associated with it must be paid back. Costs are low provided you do not require leverage. In fact, the costs are similar to other retirement plans. The tax advantages are excellent, but it will require the help of several enlightened advisors to get the job done.

Chapter

13

BUSINESS
EXIT
PLAN
VISITED

BUSINESS EXIT PLAN VISITED

Recently I have met with several business owners who don't have a clue as to how they will sell their business or what the value might be in the open market. When I ask what their time horizon is for exiting the business, I get a response similar to the one from a newlywed couple when asked about having children. "Oh, in about five years sounds right." Maybe you are of the mindset that you simply take the recent multiples of other sales in your industry and sell for the same. There are lots of variables to consider beyond industry standards or formulas. Having a conversation with a skilled professional is a great place to start. Another resource is your trade associations and the professionals that work your market. Too often we find the reasoning to be too simplistic when approaching the sale of a business. Getting the $5 million price tag and carrying the note may turn into a disaster. Getting $4 million cash or a combination of stock swap and cash may in fact work best. Just because there is a price tag that sounds right may not help you keep more in your pocket. Talking with an accountant about the exit plan is very important to get clear on the differing tax rates on different assets when sold. The structure or the type of deal where you pay a lower tax rate depends on a lot of variables. Are you of the mindset that inventories are taxed the same as, say, goodwill or capital equipment? They are not taxed the same nor are the rules in which you deal with recapture of depreciation. Some industries get special breaks in the area of taxes on some items. If you missed the material on Employee Stock Ownership Plans, then by all means go back and read it.

Some of the goals generally sought by owner management are: providing income during retirement, minimizing estate and gift tax liability, preserving the "ongoing concern" value of the business, providing enough liquidity during retirement and at death to satisfy debts and taxes.

We saw a national survey review which showed that 70% of closely held businesses are likely to become part of the Chief Executive Officer's estate and that 40% of all closely-held corporations will face serious estate and succession problems in the next ten years. The reasons for serious issues stem from lack of preparation in the area of liquidity, management beyond the CEO/owner, and lack of systems: accounting, process, and contingency plans. It would be a great idea to start the first day and have an exit plan in mind for either death or disability or eventual retirement. In reality, this almost never happens.

What are you going to do next? We have seen individuals who have poured themselves into a business for decades and upon selling the business either die or get very critical and sour. However, those with purpose outside of the business, such as high involvement in family, fare very well in the transition. Transitional management is a term used for coaching individuals in this often-stressful process.

A business intermediary friend of mine shared with me a simple case of how a business owner had not figured in benefits to the shareholder. The business owner had membership at an exclusive club with golf and tennis privileges and wonderful meals to court prospective clients. He had two company autos for himself and his spouse for travel. Many of the industry trips were in exciting locations and the time was well spent learning from others in the business and getting some time away to get refreshed. Many vendors of the company provided free advice and little benefits that really added up over time. Having the choice of which vendors to purchase from also created some other opportunities for the family to get employment for the children and other benefits not available to everyone. Example: A vendor calls to provide tickets to a major league baseball game that was sold out and with box seats, a parking pass and personal introductions to the teams' coaches. How does one value all these benefits and opportunities? Can you see where this is heading? One, if the new owner could also add back the expenses to net profit and then make his own choices based on his preferences, then that would be a start. Next, if there were unique assets in the form of special relationships and special event venues that were carried with the business, then what value would the new owner place on those assets? Think about special items that would in fact go away for both you and your family if you sold today. Would it matter to your family and is that important to you? One business owner told me he wanted to get rid of the easy gravy train his son was accustomed to and wanted his son to either go get another real job or learn how to deal in the real world of produce or perish.

Determination of whom to sell to? One of three potential buyers: family, those within the business and, lastly, those outside the business.

What are the Risks when selling to the Insider vs. Outsider? Can an insider be strong enough to complete the deal and carry the company forward? One very important consideration is if the likely buyer is an outsider publicly traded firm, then it will behoove you to spend the extra money today on your accounting and get your books in alignment with a public firm's records. Otherwise it will delay the process and cost you later to go back and pay for and wait to have good records. It has also opened up doors to have such a firm promote you to others as one possible method of marketing the firm. Law firms involved in lots of business transactions are another good potential source to market the sale of your business. Often we hear that it is best to set up and run your business as if you were in the market to sell it the first day you start and you will make wiser decisions towards maximizing the value of the business.

The art of the deal: Get the right terms to meet your clearly laid out objectives and placing a price on the risk you assume. Again, the team you employ at this time can make a powerful impact. Scary thought: You sell for the stated price with earn out and a promissory note and the new owner is weak and losing clients and trashing the business. What good is the promissory note of a bankrupt business owner or what is the possibility of paying you all you are due on low earn out? Take them to court and deal with the courts and rules while the business runs down? Not a good retirement plan in anybody's world.

Details to address before you exit: Having a tax plan vs. having the government plan their collection of your hard earned proceeds by default are two very different paths and the choice is yours with enlightened advisors guiding you. If you are away from the business a lot, maybe you should consider bringing in an outsider to run the company and grow it while you handle only one aspect of the business that you are the best at, such as sales or networking. We see this as one of the more viable methods. Get someone better than yourself in a particular area like administration and then you get focused on doing what are your best skills. Often, each one of us may have really strong skills in technical aspects or marketing or team building. What would your perfect day look like? What things would you be doing or not be doing? Where would you invest your time and energy and focus if you were not doing what you are doing today? Often we get "I guess I would be on a sailboat in the Caribbean or on the golf course every day." These responses lack passion and specific direction to really take over as the guiding light if one of these individuals were to strike it rich and sell out or win through another windfall. Why not get coaching now to determine specifically what you want to do for the rest of your life and how you would like to design the journey? If not, then circumstances and opportunities will likely direct the path. We see some business owners sell or retire and become critical and rude and disillusioned with the whole concept of taking it easy. Having a personal life coach ask you well-positioned questions will open up what is possible for you and what you can design and achieve during those years after exiting the business. Take time to write down the three things you would most like to do right now and see if this could be accomplished while you are still working and earning and providing benefits to others.

Even if you do not plan to sell anytime soon, you should address a proper buy/sell agreement if another company or individual lined up to buy in order to protect the family's value in the business. Having an agreement helps to fix a price for estate tax purposes. The IRS provides the following rules when dealing with estate tax: 1) The agreement cannot be a device to transfer property to a member of the decedent's family for less than full and adequate consideration in money or money's worth. 2) The agreement must represent a bona fide business arrangement, and 3) its terms must be comparable to similar agreements entered into in an arms-length agreement. Arms-length would exclude family members and other related companies.

Chapter 14

THE
NOBLEMAN'S
ARMY

THE NOBLEMAN'S ARMY

Most of us have heard, while growing up, the story of Robin Hood and his merry men. Some say this is a political story of how the government should redistribute wealth or at least attempt some social engineering. Others say it's just a story of having fun with the adventure of taking care of the underdog. Something inside most of us calls out and thinks the idea is great so long as Robin Hood or the Government is not targeting us. Either way, there is something to be learned from the story. The rich nobleman, next time he travels around Sherwood Forest, takes an army to protect himself and his possessions from those would-be thieves called Robin Hood.

Who are these protectors or hired armies that surround the modern day businessman? They are the accountant, attorney, financial advisor, insurance agent, and others hired to perform modern functions and tactics of financial and legal battle. What might the tactics include and why use them?

The first line of defense for many is the accountant because of frequent communications regarding business and personal taxes. What are the tactics typically employed by the Man of Means? Consider several little things that can add up to be a significant number. Little things like matching up the passive activity losses with passive gains, finding methods to reduce Medicare taxes, options in selling off assets vs. selling off stock positions. Another issue that warrants a good review is the Research and Development Tax Credit. It is like a coupon against taxes. Many only see this for manufacturing and yet there are lots of other industries that may qualify. This is not a tax exercise or accounting exercise, rather a team approach to get this valuable benefit. You have taken tax deductions for these costs and you could be eligible to take another 6% credit off of your taxes, not off of your income. This is not automatic. You have to qualify and you have to apply. By the way, the form is only one page and likely you have all the documentation necessary. Cost Segregation is another area. This is accelerated deprecation on investment property. There is the potential for tens of thousands of dollars or more in your pocket today rather than years from now.

Another obvious protector is that of the attorney: real estate attorneys for the transactions and often for the protective structures to hold such property. Estate planning attorneys can do a lot more than provide protections from the vultures of the government. By the way, estate taxes are called voluntary taxes. We as taxpayers elect to divert to taxable buckets or to non-taxable buckets. The non-taxable buckets are charities, donor advised funds or private family foundations. "A Donor Advised Fund offers the opportunity to create an easy-to-establish, low cost, flexible vehicle for charitable giving." Private Family Foundation is a charity, but it is not a public charity nor a supporting organization.

Asset protection attorneys are a growing portion of either very large firms with many wealthy clients or estate planning boutiques with a designated individual to specialize. In our opinion they should be well versed in the opportunities within both domestic and offshore asset protection trusts. They should become very familiar with private placement life policies and how the rules work as to diversification of private investments and special provisions. Some policies offer greater flexibility such as in-kind premium payment, 1035 exchange rules, and loan provisions. Because they work with wealthy business people and some with very large potential liabilities, they should know various ways to structure the companies to benefit not only the protection side today but act in a favorable way in the future with estate planning, gifting and business disposition. A successful plan not only should provide ultimate protection but should also help in discouraging any lawsuits up front. It should take away the nuisance of frivolous lawsuits and the time, energy and money it takes to even address the charge or claim.

Financial advisors have lots of resources available and are often the ones with the most cutting edge concepts due to advanced planning services, alternative investments, insurance training, and creative investment product vendors. Some have advanced risk management experience such as put options, equity collars, and asset protection planning and risk analysis.

One of the more overlooked professionals we all need to utilize more is the property and casualty agent. Having one that asks lots of questions to best suit your needs and desires is critical to long-term financial health. Recently, I had a conversation about an often missed coverage, that of "Employment Practices Liability" a.k.a. EPL. EPL is not cheap and for two reasons: One is the high likelihood of claim in today's litigious environment. For the disgruntled employee, this is equal to near guaranteed lottery winnings. Second is the fact that so few employers know of this valuable coverage and those that are made aware of it find it too expensive relative to other coverages.

Life & health agents should be a great resource in that they ask the tough questions for each of us to be accountable to our commitments to family and others. This is a place where we need to be responsible and not overdo it, shifting the majority of one income into insurance premiums. Do you still need coverage when your assets are large enough to take care of the family? What is the purpose for the coverage? What are the critical elements of your health coverage?

What to expect from an enlightened financial advisor is the following: Assess risk in portfolio of investments, determine where on the path to stated financial goals one is positioned, risk transfers and when and how to do them, estate planning basics and, in some cases, extensive planning to maximize asset transfer and tax reduction strategies today and for future generations, investment and cash flow management, and an overall plan fit for meeting goals. Use your enlighten advisor and be bold in questioning them about the strategies they recommend.

Chapter 15

COLLABORATION

Collaboration

What happens when you do not do it? What happens when you do? Can optimal results be consistent without collaboration? I would venture to say it would be impossible. With effective collaboration the level of communication is at such a place that clear and compelling results are not only likely but the normal result. Not guaranteed; however, so compelling that it will draw your advisors back to the process and they will forever attempt to repeat the success. Without training and real effort to apply these processes the chance of repeat performance without the proper training will likely not happen.

The components

> What High Net-Worth Individuals Want
> Well-Organized Team
> Access Online
> Education
> Solutions, not Products
> Empowerment

It's about being client-centered and having the skills and ability to get along with and work with others' strengths.

The SWOT Method is widely used in the military as a decision-making process.

Strengths, Weakness, Opportunities, and Threats are a framework to address the issue at hand and get clarity.

Here is what happens when not doing it right.
Most advisors think collaboration is really only a sharing of information as necessary. What that looks like is a disconnected conversation and no real working together to get clear on the client's objectives. More of a plan to get done what each advisor brings to the table such as a product or service. See the graph below which shows all arrows facing to the right and advisor A refers to advisor B and provides a little background on the client and then B hands off to advisor C who doesn't know what A did and little or none of what B has performed. The process continues with disconnected conversations and while each of the advisors may talk in passing or they may in fact know each other well, the process is lacking the key element of client-centered coordination.

In India there is a story about the five blind men who had been blind since birth and had never heard the description of an elephant and had never encountered such an animal. They were all brought together and the very wise rajah asked each of them to describe his first encounter with the elephant. Each was introduced separately to the creature and then one by one they shared with the group the details. The first had the trunk, the next the side, the next the tail, the next ear, the next legs. As each described only the portion he experienced, they began to argue with one another. The first said it was like a big strong snake, the next, no, it's like a large wall, solid and strong, no, it's like a rope that wiggles, no, it's like a soft fan producing a gentle breeze, no, it's like a tree firmly planted. The rajah allowed the arguing to continue a little while then stopped the blind men and told them they all were correct in describing the huge creature and that they needed to get together in order to better understand the whole elephant. It's like that for advisors to see the elephant. The solution is not about the limited aspect of tax code, or legal documents or insurance or financial products. It's about understanding the client and the bigger picture and seeing clearly the solutions from others perspectives.

WealthCycles' Process Template

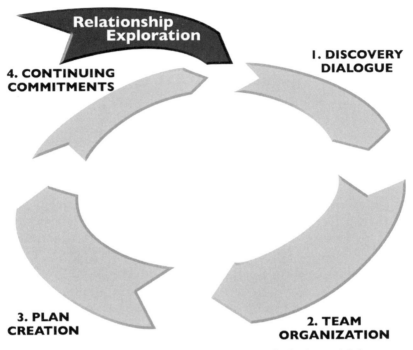

Relationship Exploration

1. DISCOVERY DIALOGUE

4. CONTINUING COMMITMENTS

3. PLAN CREATION

2. TEAM ORGANIZATION

Used with the permission of Co-Act Solutions, LLC

Discovery Dialogue:

This is where the advisors review "Who we are, what we do, and how we do it." Gathering and updating data and identifying existing relationships with advisors.

Team Organization:

The creation and refinement of membership of the Collaborative Team that will assist. The team may be as simple as one person or several disciplines all working together.

Plan Creation:

The team creates, presents and implements the client plan. Having a lead member that knows how to assign tasks and track follow up sets apart the process from traditional methods.

Continuing Commitment:

There is a process to provide the entire team with tools and support essential to a long and mutually beneficial client-team relationship. This completes the cycle and prepares for a new cycle. Here we find period plan evaluations, legacy planning and team development support.

It starts with setting the expectations and gaining agreement from you the client in regard to the main issues. Explain the process of collaboration and find out who are the advisors and then qualify them as to whether they will be appropriate for the team. It's not about sharing of revenues or splitting fees and commissions, but rather working as a team of professionals to get done what needs to be accomplished according to the client and his issues. The lead collaborator should be able to facilitate and communicate with an agenda set forth by you the client. Each advisor should feel open and trusting of each other and the process. The client is the boss always and if someone is whining about something and it's not appropriate, then it will be obvious. Every client has unique issues and the advisors will discover that it's not about, "This looks familiar, and therefore this is the solution based on the last similar looking case." As you read this, we hope it will become apparent that as the client you have a responsibility to open up and discuss concerns and issues freely with your trusted advisors. Often while attending these collaborating meetings, usually with estate planning attorneys, we discover the real drivers and passions so that when it's all over, we know what is most important. What are the causes or programs or people that mean the most to those we are assisting and planning with so diligently? This can make all the difference, knowing truly what the priorities are and then planning in accordance with those items.

The result desired is consistent and excellent interaction and best results when all are working for the client's best interests. This should be clearly demonstrated and applied to each advisor's role. There must be clear understanding up front on roles and compensation, with the objectives guiding the focus of each.

Facilitating Questions during the discovery dialogue. Start with: What are the issues you are trying to address? Which of these is most important and why? When would you like to see this accomplished and what are you willing to do to get this accomplished? If given the choice of doing anything in the world and money was no object what would it be and why would you do it? What expectations do you have in terms of fees, time and energy to accomplish your goals? Have you given thought to the preferred method by which you would like to approach the issue at hand? Would you like your advisors to see this as primarily the way to look over all other issues? What advisors have you utilized in solving the issue in the past and how did that work out? Whom do you consider to be your current advisors and have they discussed the issue with you? If not, then why not? If so, then what did you like best about their approach and recommendations? Have you given up hope on getting a solution?

What is the issue? How long has this been an issue? What have you tried? How did that work out for you? Do you have some new insights on how you would approach this issue? How much do you expect this issue has cost you in terms of money, time, and stress? Have you given up hope? What would you expect to invest here to get the issue resolved? If you could describe a perfect world or ideal way to have this take place for you, what would it look like? What might be a realistic time frame to resolve the issue?

Case Study of how team members become better in this clear environment and the client knows exactly the agenda and purpose of meetings. It works great online, over phone and in person. Logistically, often it is difficult to get all the parties together, yet online and conference call should be the objective when meeting in person is too difficult.

What would an online meeting look like and what kind of a leadership management is most effective? Large corporations make management decisions at the department level with direction from the top to coordinate.

Whom would you not include in the process of collaboration? Who should be involved in the process? Who should set the framework and agenda and direct the meetings? It would be nice if the client had knowledge to get things done and knew how to get each of the advisors focused on tasks at hand and open to the ideas of each and willing to explore.

You, the Man of Means, are in the best position to set the objective, to facilitate the advisor team; after all, it is your money. However, you may not be in the best position to separate friendships and emotions for facilitating a team. For example, advisor B is Joe your close friend. He's a confident life insurance agent that believes insurance buys are the best answer and most appropriate fit for the majority of your money. Paul is your longtime investment advisor and is quick to point out the limitations and cost of focusing too heavily on insurance solutions. Paul may not understand conservative viewpoints regarding risk management. Therefore, they will argue their points emphatically, wasting your time. Just like the metaphorical story of the five blind men experiencing the elephant for the first time. This could limit the chance of a good plan from going forward. Therefore a solution may be to elect a different facilitator to implement your objectives. This may be a CPA, an attorney, or a wealth adviser who can follow your objectives in facilitating the team. You want to have an adviser who will clearly set the agenda for the other advisers and keep your plan on track.

Checklist:

Leave ego at the door.
Different views are a positive.
Different skills among advisors to fit the need.
Define the process upfront.
Critical for client input upfront.

Advisors should work within a planned process and communicate with facts based on the clear objectives of the client. Not all advisors are required to be in all the meetings. On the other hand, having a team that communicates often regarding such planning and will update all those involved will greatly enhance the process and continuity of the plan. It helps to have a process and agenda and technology to facilitate the online meetings.

Appendix

A CHEAP DATE

Thomas Stanley, author of *The Millionaire Mind* and *The Millionaire Next Door*, says the to sum up the makeup of those in the studies, the three words that best describe those interviewed are: "A Cheap Date."

The activities they expressed as most important were (1) spending time with family, sitting and eating and hanging out and (2) having time with friends like bridge or garden clubs or having others over for dinner.

We have compiled a list of cheap dates we would like to share with you.

Ideas for a Cheap Date
for your family or just the two of you:

1. Go to the beach for the day and take refreshments. Refrain from buying at the high margin vendors. Enjoy walking, swimming, the sand, or a book in the shade.

2. Picnic at a state or city park. Enjoy walking, music, relaxing, or perhaps throwing a ball.

3. Canoe or paddleboat. Take refreshments and seek advice on different spots to visit and explore.

4. A city concert or parade often provides hours of fun. Go prepared with folding chairs and drinks.

5. Play putt-putt golf or, better yet, go to a driving range and get a bucket of balls. Practice chips and putts.

6. One that my children enjoy: Go for donuts or bagels, or a drive-thru for breakfast. Then head for the airport to eat and watch planes take off and land.

7. A charity auction. There are bargains on some items; know the value. It's even more fun if you believe in the cause and can mix with like-minded people.

8. If you have a dog, take it to a dog park if there is one in your area, or boating with you.

9. Another one popular with my kids is riding a city bus to some place to get a treat.

10. Utilize your gym membership to work out and take advantage of the childcare and exercise classes.

11. Go to one of the "Village" centers, get an ice cream cone and window shop. (After the stores close or it could get expensive!)

12. Get your library's schedule for children's activities, or just go without them, and spend an afternoon at the library browsing.

13. Hang out downtown, feed the swans and watch the people!

14. If you don't have a team, "adopt" a nearby high school and go to home games – soccer, basketball, football, track meet, etc.

15. Explore the museums in your area and get to know local free events such as art and craft shows etc.

16. Consider joining a house of faith like a church or synagogue.

17. If you have a local college or university they can provide lectures on lots of interesting topics or entertaining venues.

18. My parents enjoy walking at the mall and sitting and watching people.

19. Fly a kite or electric airplane at a local school field.

20. Join a sports team such as a city league, church league or company team in tennis, bowling, softball or soccer league.

21. Hit a bucket of balls on the putting green, sand trap or driving range.

22. Enrichment classes offered at church or community schools.

23. Some businesses offer classes such as dance, sewing, cooking, crafts, photography or painting, or woodworking as an extension of the services they sell.

24. Hike the local trails and take in the beauty of nature.

25. If you have a talent like singing, then be part of a choir.

OUTSOURCE

Outsourcing can be little things such as dictation service recorded and e-mailed back to you the same day or having computer techs on standby with guaranteed service within a certain period of time. Outsourcing services such as payroll relieves you of potential liabilities and headaches associated with governmental regulations. Another step would be to integrate a Professional Employee Organization, aka PEO, outsource to take on benefits, regulations, insurance and human resource functions. We see friends that broker in this area and they are tremendous in helping find savings and benefits to be realized if matched up with the proper PEO. PEOs can be a great value and easy way to gain access to lots of resources. One caveat here is many of these programs can potentially limit you as the owner-employer on taking benefits for yourself. An example would be VEBA setup for your company, not in a PEO arrangement, which could set up very significant funding for future medicals and, if it is part of a large PEO, then benefits could be more diluted when combined. Another example would be in the area of a Defined Benefit Plan and the types of investments or investment manager choices are usually more restricted.

We see too that often if you, as the employer, went to XYZ PEO Company and if you are not a perfect fit for them, then it might be like going to a shoe store that only sells wide sizes. So what do they say if you are a

regular foot? Wear thicker socks, tighten the strings or wash them and dry them. You get the point.
Here are benefits found in using a PEO:

Core Services of a PEO

<u>Human Resources Management and Support</u>

New Client Orientation
Fair Labor Standards Act Compliance (FLSA)
Wage and Hour Review of Human Resources Practices
Worksite Employee Handbook
Employment Practice Liability Insurance * offered by some PEOs
General Worksite Employee Relations Issues
Record Keeping and File Maintenance
Worksite Employee Separation Assistance
Unemployment Compensation Claims Management
Equal Employment Opportunity (EEO) Compliance
The Family Medical Leave Act (FMLA)
Fair Labor Standards Act Compliance (FLSA)
Child Labor Compliance

<u>Payroll Services</u>

The National Labor Relations Act (NLRA) Payroll and Tax Processing
Payroll Processing- Online
Internet Access and Time Entry via the Web
Garnishments
W-2s
Online Payroll Reports
Worksite Employee Pay Options
Tax Deposits
Quarterly Federal and State Tax Withholding
State Unemployment Rate Management
Compliance and Reporting

Tip Tax Credit

Workers Compensation Insurance Management

Safety and Loss Control
On-Line Safety Training and Materials
OSHA Compliance Instruction
Assistance with OSHA Abatement
Recommendations on safe workplace and best practices
Train-the-Trainer Programs
Accident Investigation
Loss Analysis with recommendations
Customized Health and Safety program
Safe Driving Policy
Workers Compensation Claims Management
State required notice of injury filing
Three-point contact
Hand selected treatment provider assignment
Claim monitored through closure
Daily on-line communication with insurance carrier
Employee drug testing (if required)
Pursuing any reductions in indemnity payments that are allowable by law
Assisting to ensure lower claim cost and promote a safe working environment.

Worksite Employee Benefits

Comprehensive Large Group Health and Welfare benefits including:
Medical
Dental
Short and Long Term Disability
Cancer Care
Payroll Deducted Auto Insurance
Discounted Movie and Theme Parks
Federal Consolidated Omnibus Budget Reconciliation Act (COBRA)

Section 125 Cafeteria Plan
Flex Plans Enrollment and Administration
401k plans and Administration or IRA for
smaller Employer groups

Let's assume you are a small employer. To outsource
a virtual assistant may, in fact, allow you the leverage
of time and flexible arrangement to make you very
productive and you would not need to provide normal
benefits associated with employee costs such as health
coverage and retirement plans.

When working with a Property and Causality agent
or broker, learn to ask the important questions about
covering all the risks and the benefits of getting a team
to work hard on the regulations and rules that are so
complicated today. If your enlightened advisors are
recommending a PEO, then be sure to hear them out
and get on it today. Some PEOs offer automatic
Employment Practice Liability coverage at no additional
cost or for a very modest fee.

GOD'S MATH

God's Math. Do we have something better to think of in terms of returns? We believe there is a return example in nature to challenge us all to rethink returns and the power of creation. Nature at its core screams out to be abundant and expand beyond our comprehension. Let's look at a few examples: Seed provides exponential growth beyond anything we see in the financial markets. My boys love to plant mammoth sunflower seeds in February in Florida. We purchase a packet of about three dozen seeds for $1 from a discount store. Next we plant them in a tray of potting soil to give them a great start and they sprout in about a week to 10 days. About three weeks later, we plant each plant in the garden area and water. About two months later we have about three dozen large plants from 6 feet tall to 15 feet tall and each head produces about 2000 seeds over about a three-month period. So $1 allowed us to do what God can do in nature, producing 72,000 seeds, and if we then had the land and labor to place these seeds in the ground and duplicate the process again over the next three months or so, we could produce 144,000,000 seeds. Should we do this again, voila!— now 28,800,000,000 in less than one year on a $1 investment and if we sold these at a wholesale cost of 50 cents for 36, then we could make $400,000,000 on a dollar's investment, in theory.

Okay, let's try another example on how nature produces big results: animal reproduction. Consider two frogs, or fish or rabbits coming together in the reproduction process and we see two become 10, 50, or 200 fertilized eggs. The gestation period for small creatures is short and within a short period of time (six weeks) their offspring will be able to produce as well. Two become thousands, in theory, over a two-year period.

Propagation example: Ivy pinched off and replanted to produce several plants. While I was visiting a friend of mine, he showed me his greenhouses full of thousands of ivy plants. I asked him about a beautiful ivy and he shared with me that he had purchased three plants about two years before from a discount store for a total of $10 and the thousands of plants I was admiring were all taken as cuttings from those three original plants. He had already sold over a thousand plants at a wholesale price of $2, as well. We talked about the costs of pots and soil and summed up that these returns were for him low risk, high reward and, yes, he gave God the credit for the return.

We share this with you to see what is possible. God's handiwork in nature ought to expand the brain to think of creative possibilities and their power. God's handiwork is alive and working well in your brain and it allows you and me to create something from nothing. The first example that comes to mind is that of an artist with a blank canvas or how a musician creates a song out of his head. Others take junk or discarded items and make something beautiful out of them. We see software vendors take ideas and create a process to map or to crunch out solutions so we can be more productive. We see managers take several individuals and get them working as a team and accomplishing great things with big results. What written text and recorded images strategically placed would produce large gains in business? Having effective marketing with little effort, driving sales in your business, may in fact become your best investment. Just as the $12 canvas with effort from the artist creates a painting worth thousands of dollars and later copies selling over the Internet 24/7 become the artist's best investment yield. Having growth that can occur day in a day out like my tree farm and its beautiful biological growth year round day after day without my involvement. By the way, trees not only grow in value, they convert carbon dioxide into oxygen. What a great investment! It makes money and makes all our lives better.

The Power of Journaling

Initially, I was not going to include my views on journaling. At the urging of others, however, I am including a few ideas that will help a few of you. Journaling is not about recording my diary entries. Journaling is capturing a moving quote, capturing the essence of a powerful speech or sermon. I found that listening improves generally and I can reference back to my journal and work out thoughts. I was not taught to journal growing up and the thought of keeping my thoughts on paper flat out scared me. What if somebody got hold of it and used it to embarrass me! Ouch. That would be painful and not something I would risk growing up. So what got me started? Simply, there was pain in my life that I needed to address and face up to. Jim Rohn, a motivational speaker and writer, got me started. He said if you don't capture it on paper then it will likely be lost forever. He talked about the idea that if you keep doing the same things over and over and expect different results, then it's insanity. He challenged me to make this year the best year ever. I took it on and, yes, it was the best year ever. But do you know what else happened? The year after that was the best year and the following year better and now ten years later I can say this is the best year ever again.

Another thing. When I met Jim Rohn, he showed me his journal and it was a nice leather bound, worn-on-the-edges, well-used book. He said, spend some money on a nice book so you will feel that you must write down important stuff and value it more highly. He was right about this, too. I buy acid free lined pages with high quality leather and gold gilded pages. I value my journals over most other books in my library and revisit them periodically. What does this have to do it with advanced tax strategies and vision and long term planning? Everything. Some of you reading this will never know if it will work for you unless you give it a real effort and pour yourself into "your journal."

My last thought here on journaling: Some people try to carry multiple journals around depending on the speaker they are going to listen to or the type of meeting they attend. I have found using one journal and starting from the beginning and addressing business and commerce issues from front to back and then starting on the last page and addressing spiritual and personal issues and working forward to meet in the middle somewhere works especially well for me.

Some of you are not at all interested in typing or writing in a journal, but you find the benefits of dictation into a digital recorder. One computer program that allows you to talk and dictate your journaling is called "Speak Naturally."

Louis Agazziz once said, "A pencil is one of the best of eyes." Think about this next statement: The greatest time waster in our lives is the time we spend undoing that which ought not to have been done in the first place. Would you agree? Do you have a compass to keep you and your family on track?

The Electronic Journal

The Electronic Journal is easy to set up in Microsoft Word. The idea is to put all the information you use (or where to get it) into one place where you can find it quickly. Open a new Word document. Under the heading "My Journal," type a list of section titles, each on a separate line with a few spaces in between. Assign them each a "Heading 1" style separately. Under each section title, fill in content, making sure the style is "normal." You can type in or Copy and Paste other text files, website links, and hyperlinks. The important part is the Table of Contents. To set up the TOC, place your cursor at the end of the line titled "My Journal," and press the Enter key twice to insert two blank lines. Choose Insert, then Reference, then Index & Tables. A dialog box will appear. Click on the "Table of Contents" tab, and then on "OK." Word will create a table of contents using your section headings that you formatted as "Heading 1." To go to a section in your Electronic Journal, place your cursor over the heading in the TOC that you want to go to. You will be able to either click on the heading and it will take you there, or you will have to press Ctrl and then click. To update the Table of Contents, right click or press F9 anywhere on the TOC. You will get the option of Updating Page Numbers or Updating Entire Table. Word will automatically update the TOC.

PREVENT FRAUD
IN YOUR COMPANY

The following is a list of items to have in place in order to reduce your risk. While talking with an attorney in Florida, I learned that a "bookkeeper" got him for more than $150,000 over a two-year period. This represented about 15% of his collected billings and she did this in the form of checks written to bogus insurance carriers, personal use of the corporate credit card and a bogus investigation company she set up. He told me that another attorney she had worked for let her go after suspecting she was taking his money. Another friend of mine had a bookkeeper for an interior design company who was very lax in accounting and books and had several hundred thousand dollars in expenses unaccounted for in the business. It was very difficult to prosecute the bookkeeper and, by the time this was apparent, the bookkeeper had left and declared bankruptcy. You know our government was set up with a check and balance system. However, it still requires each of us to hold those elected accountable and vote to replace them when issues surface.

According to a 2006 Report to the Nation on Occupational Fraud & Abuse, ACFE: "The medium loss for a business with fewer than 100 employees was $190,000 per fraud scheme." The report goes on to say that an estimated 5% of annual revenues are lost to fraud. Multiply that times the GNP and now hundreds of billions. We hear about the big cases of fraud like WorldCom & Enron and yet the little stuff goes

unreported in the media.
Here are a few simple changes to consider:

1. Set the tone at the top.

2. Create an anonymous fraud hotline and publicly emphasize to your staff how important it is for everyone to join the fight against fraud. Assure employees that the hotline is anonymous and that they will be protected from retaliation.

3. Communicate your intentions to strengthen internal controls (which might include surprise audits).

4. Host fraud training sessions to emphasize that fraud will not be tolerated and that the consequences of fraud impact everyone.

5. Be the first person to open bank statements. Scan the transactions that have cleared the bank and review the enclosed checks for unusual activity.

6. Consider personally signing all checks.

7. Take note of what is happening around you both inside and outside the office. Look for odd work schedules, staying late, coming in early, or working weekends. Has there been a noticeable change in an individual's lifestyle (e.g. extravagant vacations, new vehicles, or jewelry)? Is someone experiencing a significant amount of stress outside of work that may also indicate a personal financial struggle (e.g. divorce, loss of spouse's job, or serious health problems)?

ABOUT THE AUTHOR

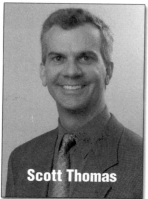

Scott Thomas

Scott Thomas is the founder of *The Financial Farmer, Inc.*, a wealth advisory firm in Orlando Florida. A registered representative and associate investment advisor of QA3 Financial Corporation of Omaha, Scott is also a Chartered Financial Consultant through The American College and a Certified Wealth Preservation Planner and Certified Asset Protection Planner through the Wealth Preservation Institute. His motto is *"to become more so I can be more for the others in my life."* Scott loves to speak to groups of successful business people regarding risks and opportunities that few ever knew existed for smaller companies, such as being responsible and having a proactive tax plan and exit plan and what it takes to be the "man of means". A common comment among those that hear Scott speak is of his ability to take complex ideas and make them easy to understand.

Scott is a proud and devoted father of three wonderful children and has been married to Suzanne for 19 years. He possesses a B.S. Degree from The University of Central Florida and is an active member in both his Rotary club and church.